COLOR FORECASTING FOR FASHION

Published in 2012 by
Laurence King Publishing Ltd
361–373 City Road, London,
EC1V 1LR, United Kingdom
T +44 20 7841 6900
F +44 20 7841 6910
enquiries@laurenceking.com
www.laurenceking.com

Text © 2012 Kate Scully and
Debra Johnston Cobb
This book was designed and produced by
Laurence King Publishing Ltd, London.

A catalog record for this book is available
from the British Library

ISBN: 978 1 85669 820 7

Senior Editor Zoe Antoniou
Development Editor Anne Townley

Design by Melanie Mues,
Mues Design, London

Page 4: Phillip Lim, Spring/Summer
collection 2010

Printed in China

COLOR
FORECASTING
FOR FASHION

KATE SCULLY   DEBRA JOHNSTON COBB

LAURENCE KING PUBLISHING

CONTENTS

INTRODUCTION

CHAPTER 1
WHAT IS COLOR FORECASTING? 8

CHAPTER 2
WHY AND HOW HAS COLOR
FORECASTING EVOLVED? 34

Related study material is available
on the Laurence King website at
www.laurenceking.com

Color evokes an emotional response,
making it a powerful tool in the
marketing of consumer products.

INTRODUCTION:
WHY WE STUDY COLOR FORECASTING

Ever since the Industrial Revolution began bringing consumers an expanding array of goods and products to choose from, color has become increasingly important in the development, marketing, and sales of those goods. This is especially true for the fashion business. Thanks to today's highly sophisticated, mass-produced, and multinational industry the consumer has become accustomed to a wide range of inspirational color choices in apparel. According to the International Colour Authority, "Color comes before style and price, and is the first factor to which the customer responds."

But just how does a brand or retailer ascertain the right color, or palette of colors, for their products? What is the process by which designers, product development teams, and buyers choose color—and where do those colors come from?

Color forecasting is the process of predicting the probable color and trend directions across the spectrum of fashion and related consumer products. It provides direction for designers, product developers, and retailers, assisting them in choosing colors that will appeal to the customer and drive sales. The role of color forecasting—researching, predicting, and ultimately interpreting color in order to drive sales of a product—has evolved as a legitimate and necessary enterprise, and one that the student of fashion design, product development, or fashion marketing and promotion needs to understand.

While color forecasting involves a great deal of research, it is also a creative process and should be an enjoyable one. Unfortunately, for many of us the concept of color forecasting can be uncomfortable, implying guesswork and an element of risk. This book aims to demystify color forecasting by exploring why and how seasonal palettes are developed. Combining their experiences and contacts in the fashion business, the authors offer a practical guide to the skills and methodologies needed to build a timely color palette that connects with the wants and needs of consumers.

Chapter 1: What is Color Forecasting? defines color forecasting and why it is vital to the business of fashion, exploring the meaning of color to the consumer and explaining the industry's timing and development cycle.

Chapter 2 : Why and How Has Color Forecasting Evolved? looks at the history of color forecasting in apparel and the forecasting business in its current position.

Chapter 3: The Language of Color explores our perceptions of color, the evolution of color theory, and the language and tools for managing color communication.

Chapter 4: Understanding Color Cycles examines the ebb and flow of consumer preferences in fashion and looks at the factors driving fads, trends, and cycles.

Chapter 5: Color Forecasting Tools and Methodologies is a practical guide to the process of developing a seasonal palette, from observation and analysis to concept, organization, and use of color theory and cycles to build a saleable color story.

Chapter 6: Color Application shows how the forecaster's palette is then translated to the product and used in the retail setting.

Chapter 7: Intuition and Inspiration in Color Forecasting discusses the influence and effect of creativity in the forecasting process and the development and practice of intuition.

CHAPTER 1
WHAT IS COLOR
FORECASTING?

WHY DO WE NEED COLOR FORECASTING?

Color is a powerful selling tool that can affect our purchasing decisions. Imagine a world where all our retail venues—stores, marketplaces, catalogs—were filled with monochromatic product. Or a world where all consumer products were available only in black. Without the emotional appeal of color, products would be purchased primarily for utilitarian purposes.

What if the colors offered at retail were the same, year after year, season after season? Would consumers continue to buy yellow T-shirts or purple sweaters if they already had versions of these garments hanging in their closets in the exact same colors? In all likelihood, consumers would purchase the same colors over again only if the garments were on sale, or if their old garments were worn out.

Now picture an array of merchandise colored helter-skelter, without regard to season, compatibility, or customer appeal—somewhat like a clearance warehouse. While the customer may like the concept of being "spoilt for choice," the array of goods, services, and brands available to us can be overwhelming.

In his bestseller *The Tipping Point*, Malcolm Gladwell discusses the theory that our brains have only a certain capacity for random information. "As human beings, in other words, we can only handle so much information at once. Once we pass a certain boundary, we become overwhelmed."

Robyn Waters, author and former Vice-President of Trend, Design, and Product Development at Target, writes, "Too much information without editing is toxic. Too many options or choices can be confusing, which can turn your customers away." Merchandise developed and colored with a point of view that connects with the customer's heart and mind is more likely to be saleable.

Even when a color **palette** has been carefully developed and is on-trend, it may simply fail to resonate with the wants and needs of a particular customer at that moment in time. The customer may not be able to recognize or express these needs, but the purchase will not take place because the customer does not respond to the colors on offer. While taking fashion trends into consideration, good color forecasting develops color ranges or palettes appropriate to the wants and needs of the customer.

Imagine a customer shopping for apparel in an upscale store. The customer has money to spend and traditional tastes. Perhaps the clothing in store that season is in offbeat, hard-to-wear shades. The array of color may be beautifully on-trend, but does not appeal to this particular customer, who is looking for color that will not only fit with her current wardrobe, but be appropriate beyond the current season.

Color in our apparel affects the way we feel about ourselves as well as the way that others view us.

Color is the first thing we notice in a product and affects our purchasing decisions.

An unedited jumble of color can make it difficult for the customer to focus and choose what to buy.

If all clothing was the same color, retail venues would be uninspiring, and our purchases would be driven only by need.

Successful retailers such as Uniqlo understand their customers and utilize color to drive sales.

USING COLOR SUCCESSFULLY

Compare the previous case with brands and retailers that understand their customers and successfully utilize color to drive sales. Their products are available in an array of colors that not only appeal to the consumer, but seem to work together in a seasonal grouping or palette that creates a visual story, sends a message that feels consistent with the perceived brand image, and appeals to the customer's heart and mind. The colors on display are colors we want to buy and wear now. Monsoon, Accessorize, J. Crew, Uniqlo, Nike, Converse, American Apparel, Boden, Apple, Le Creuset, and cosmetics brands such as OPI and Chanel are just a few of the companies that execute color successfully.

Through correct color forecasting these brands and retailers consistently utilize color to speak to the consumer and ultimately drive sales. Their colors are carefully chosen to appeal to their particular customer base. Their palettes offer a variety of choices, but do not overwhelm. The ranges are edited so that the colors complement one another. They look new, but not too new, and they may include certain colors carried over from the last season, or **classic colors** such as black, navy, khaki, white, or gray.

Color Marketing Group, an international association for color design professionals, sums up the effect of color in their motto: "Color Sells, and the Right Colors Sell Better." The right color can make a product fly off the shelves—while the wrong color can be a very costly mistake, resulting in loss of sales, mark-downs, and returns to the manufacturer.

Color forecasting is the process of predicting the probable color and trend directions for fashion and related consumer products.

Brands and retailers use color forecasting to develop edited color ranges that offer newness and variety as well as familiar best-selling shades, all working together to encourage multiple purchases.

THE COLOR FORECASTER

At SpinExpo New York, color trends for Fall 2010 knitwear included a palette of warm reds, golds, and pinks.

Color forecasting is done by skillful and experienced individuals with an eye for color and a curiosity about almost everything. Most color forecasters have art and design training in textiles or in fashion. However, color forecasting also requires knowledge—and practice—in psychology, sociology, anthropology, marketing, art and design history, and critical analysis.

Color forecasting is also undertaken by various professional organizations, trend bureaux, trade show consortiums, and retailers' product development teams. Many color forecasters who work as freelancers or sole traders have gained experience through working for various trend consultancies. We will examine some of these organizations in Chapter 2.

Color forecasters must develop their palettes with two sets of customers in mind. The first customer is the designer, product developer, or retailer with whom the color forecaster interacts directly, and who is paying for the palette and consultation. The second and ultimate customer, of course, is the consumer, whose purchasing decisions will confirm whether or not the color forecaster has done well. The goal of the color forecaster, then, is to enable the manufacturers, brands, and retailers to provide merchandise that will appeal to consumers and promote profitable sales.

The personal likes and dislikes of the color forecaster have little to do with developing a palette, although an understanding of color and a practiced taste level are key. The conundrum is that the color forecaster will be developing a palette for the consumer long before the consumer has any idea of what colors they will want at that point in time.

COLOR FORECASTING AS A MARKETING TOOL

Some may question whether color forecasting is a professional conspiracy or a self-fulfilling prophecy in that if enough forecasters, retailers, and brands promote a trend it will become a reality, whether or not the customer is ready for it. This would suggest that forecasting is a marketing tool that pushes the consumer into a cycle of buying new products in order to be on-trend.

The reality is that good color forecasting drives sales by developing the right colors at the right time. Its goal is to create colors for products that consumers want to buy. These colors must appeal to consumers for emotional and psychological reasons. They may or may not be part of an overall seasonal trend, but they should resonate with the spirit of the times and the consumer's lifestyle.

There is still a feeling in some areas that forecasting is not a "real" business function, but for most people it is a fascinating and important area of design aesthetics, marketing, **branding**, and selling. Color strategist and trend forecaster Kate Smith tells us, "Color plays such a critical role in the success of a product or brand, and so many companies are in need of a strategy based on solid color knowledge that there is room for more people to enter this field."

Professional color forecasters such as those at Color Marketing Group have an eye for color as well as analytical skills and knowledge of consumer trends.

Color forecasting is also undertaken by trade shows such as Interfilière (shown here) and Première Vision.

The goal of the color forecaster is to create colors for products that consumers want to buy.

AN ART OR A SCIENCE?

Most people (outside of those who work in product development) have no idea how the colors we see in consumer products are developed. Where do these color palettes come from? Why do certain colors or color families sell well in a particular season, while others do not? While there is no rule or formula for the development of color, product designers do not generally choose colors on a whim. The process of forecasting shifts in consumer color preferences is actually a complex one.

Color forecasting is a creative process that requires a healthy dose of **inspiration** and **intuition**. Roseann Forde, former Global Fashion Director at DuPont (now Invista) and currently President of Fordecasting, believes that, "Intuition also plays a major role in selecting a color palette, as it is an artistic endeavor. There is that creative part of us that puts colors together in a way that is pleasing to the eye and speaks to the viewer."

Critics accuse color forecasters of "waving a magic wand" or creating color palettes out of thin air. Pat Tunsky, Creative Director of The Doneger Group, says, "I believe that you cannot pick a color palette out of a hat. I do think in many ways it is intuitive and is based on doing a lot of thinking about what the new direction in color should be and whether or not the customer is ready to accept it."

The color forecaster must learn "how to see" color in the day-to-day, as well as in broader cycles, with an understanding of color's psychological and emotional influence and how this affects consumer purchasing.

It is not always easy to measure the success level of a particular palette. Color is just one part of a product's appeal, or lack thereof. It is certainly possible for a color palette to be off, or for a forecaster to make a mistake. As we have seen, a color palette may be artistically beautiful, but may not resonate with consumers.

Color forecasting is therefore both an art and a science. The seasoned color forecaster attempts to anticipate the wants and needs of the buying public through observation and analysis of cultural trends and consumer behavior, and combines this with a creative flair for color and design, along with a strong dose of intuition and inspiration. We will examine this process more closely in Chapters 5, 6, and 7.

While color inspiration comes from artistic installations such as those at Première Vision, color forecasting also involves scientific research and analysis.

Color forecasters tune in to social and cultural trends, such as graffiti, and analyze how these will affect consumers' thinking.

By displaying their collection for Interfilière in seasonal colors, Eurojersey's fabrics resonate with the designers and buyers shopping the trade show.

©Photo Nguyen Ngoc / enn2004@free.fr

COLOR MEANING AND SYMBOLISM

Color is a shortcut that conveys a message quickly and directly without the time-consuming use of words or complex images; it grabs our attention and sends a message that can alter our perception of a product. Nowhere does this hold truer than in the apparel we choose to wear. Color in fashion can alter our moods, the way we feel about ourselves, and how others respond to us. "If fashion is a language, color is one of its main means of expression," posted Veronica Culatti on the Chromophilia blog.

The use of color to give meaning and identity to a product relies on an understanding of the messages and meanings of color, and our responses to them. Our perceptions in the natural world rely on internal memory and trigger responses that are innate and universal: blue skies and green grass are cheerful and calming, implying that the weather is benign and the crops are growing, while yellow/black stripes, dark gray clouds, or blood red signal danger.

Our understanding of and communication using color are also a result of our cultural learnings. The Cooper-Hewitt National Design Museum's "Fashion in Colors" exhibition in 2005–2006 explored this concept through a range of historical apparel. *US Vogue* editor Diana Vreeland perhaps best summed up the effect of culture on color perception in her succinct remark that "Pink is the navy blue of India."

CULTURAL DIFFERENCES

In early Christianity, yellow was the color of heretics, while in China it was historically the color of the emperor, so noble that common people were forbidden to wear it. In Western Europe, purple has always been the color of royalty, due to the rarity and price of purple dyestuffs.

Green is the sacred color of Islam, while in England it may be associated with decay and disease, as well as with fertility and new life. In the West pink is often associated with a pastel color marketed to little girls; in Asian and Hispanic cultures it can be a bright fuchsia or magenta. Khaki was originally a specific color (that of the mud of Multan, a military cantonment of British India) introduced for regimental uniforms in the 1880s. The name "khaki" is now used for a wide range of beige to tan neutrals, usually seen in casual pants (trousers). Red is a celebratory color worn by brides in much of Eastern culture, but in the West it is associated with subversive sexual behavior, as in "red light district" and "scarlet woman."

According to Jennifer Craik in her book *Fashion: The Key Concepts*, white, black, and red have the most powerful meanings across cultures and hence are the basis of most color systems. White is often associated with goodness, purity, and cleanliness, and is the color of mourning in some societies; red conjures up danger, blood, sex, fertility, liberal or leftist politics, fire and warmth, church vestments, and the devil. Black's many connotations include death (it is the color of mourning in the West), magic, secrecy, political or religious conservatism, simplicity, elegance, and luxury.

The popularity of black as the core color of fashion has its roots not only in symbolism but in its historical use and religious, political, and social connotations. In the West, the use of black in Victorian mourning dress gave way to the predominance of black for men's business suits, then became the epitome of chic in Chanel's little black dress. In contemporary times black has become the backbone of fashion because it is anonymous and asexual; many consumers choose black to fit into the mainstream and avoid making the wrong color choices. Black is also viewed by consumers as a base color in their closets, against which any and all other colors "work."

As consumers, our perceptions and use of color, therefore, are innate, cultural, and highly individual. This includes our use of color in clothing. In color forecasting a color is neither right nor wrong, but may be judged, accepted, or rejected by a particular consumer for a particular end use in a particular season. It is the understanding of the myriad wants and needs of the consumer with regard to the use of color that is at the heart of color forecasting.

Our innate understanding of color in the natural world influences our perception of yellow and black as "dangerous."

Cultural learnings influence our color preferences. In Asian cultures vivid pinks and reds are as ubiquitous as navy in the West.

The prevalence of black in our closets is rooted in historical, political, and social connotations in western culture.

At Color Marketing Group and other professional forecasting organizations, the process begins two years in advance by analyzing social, cultural, and economic trends.

COLOR FORECASTING AND CULTURAL TRENDS

Alongside the use of inspiration and intuition, the color forecaster must analyze and interpret color in the context of societal changes in order to predict consumer color preferences well in advance of the selling season.

Societal changes are shifts in the way consumers think and behave. They may be evolutionary, such as the movement for women's rights, which has changed the way men and women interact on many levels. Or they may be driven by sudden dramatic occurrences, such as the 9/11 attack on the US, which resulted in a culture shift as families drew closer, crime dropped, and strangers practiced random acts of kindness.

Societal changes can also be driven by events within the arts, sports, politics, or any of the myriad global events that we experience daily. These could be anything from an actress' dress on the red carpet, or the setting of a popular movie, to a museum exhibit, an archaeological discovery, a technological breakthrough, or the election of a new president. The color forecaster must not only be immersed in current culture but must also have an understanding of historical cultures and artistic milieus.

For example, the past decade's increased awareness of climate change and the need to preserve natural resources has driven an increase in the preference for blues and greens, the colors of air and water. The economic crisis of 2008/2009 saw a rise in the value of tangible assets such as gold, silver, and platinum—and a resurgence of metallic colors and finishes in consumer products.

Another example of a cultural trend that signaled a shift in consumer color preferences was the 2009 celebration of Charles Darwin's bicentenary. This increased our interest in nature and indigenous cultures, and a number of designers featured patterns and colorways based on natural habitats, wildlife, and native handicrafts. Colors such as jungle greens, earthy browns, and natural nude, beige, and white tones began to make an appearance.

Consumer preferences change because of, and along with, the cultural, social, political, and economic trends that add up to the general **zeitgeist**. In *The Trendmaster's Guide*, Robyn Waters describes trends as "indicators that point to what's going on in the hearts and minds of consumers"; in *The Tipping Point*, Gladwell discusses how trends begin and develop to the epidemic point. "We need to prepare ourselves for the possibility that sometimes big changes follow from small events and that sometimes these changes can happen very quickly."

Consumers related more to colors such as rain forest greens and earthy browns as society became more concerned with nature and the environment.

Recorded in a student notebook, Charles Darwin's bicentenary in 2009 increased our interest in nature and indigenous cultures.

Jungle inspired

Through observation and research, the color forecaster identifies the small and large changes in consumer lifestyles and preferences, and tracks current and emerging trends. According to Li Edelkoort, one of the world's most renowned design consultants, trend researchers do not invent trends. In an interview on the website of flavor and fragrance product developer Symrise, she says, "I don't discover anything new. I observe and interpret peoples' behavior and moods and note down what I see. I act as a catalyst for the spirit of the day."

Color evolution reflects cultural changes. But while it is one thing to observe and track societal trends, the color forecaster's true skill lies in identifying a trend early in its development, then making the connection between an emerging trend and the wants and needs of the consumer two years down the road, and translating those wants and needs into color preferences. The color forecaster must see and understand a cultural trend *before* it reaches what Gladwell calls the **tipping point**: "the moment of critical mass, the threshold, the boiling point."

It is the color forecaster's job to catch an emerging cultural trend, analyze it in terms of the consumer's future wants and needs, translate this information into a color direction through an understanding of color's emotional and psychological meanings, and create a workable palette that is pleasing to the eye and will have message and meaning for designers and product developers.

If successful, this process enables manufacturers, brands, and retailers to provide merchandise that will appeal to consumers and promote profitable sales.

Seasonal palettes such as these from PANTONE® VIEW Colour Planner are developed for the fashion industry based on consumer trends.

Here the color forecaster captures consumers' growing interest in Darwin and ecology with a palette called "Galapagos."

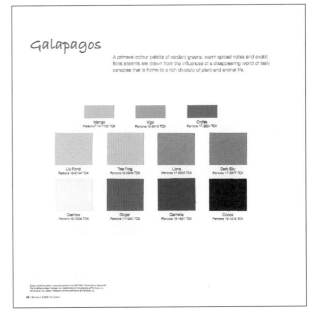

Galapagos

A primeval colour palette of verdant greens, warm spiced notes and exotic floral accents are drawn from the influences of a disappearing world of leafy canopies that is home to a rich diversity of plant and animal life.

Mango Pantone 14-1135 TCX	Vigo Pantone 16-0416 TCX	Orchis Pantone 17-2624 TCX
Lily Pond Pantone 19-6114 TCX	Tree Frog Pantone 16-0948 TCX	Liana Pantone 17-0535 TCX	Dark Sky Pantone 17-3917 TCX
Cashew Pantone 12-0304 TCX	Ginger Pantone 17-1340 TCX	Carmine Pantone 18-1631 TCX	Cocoa Pantone 19-1218 TCX

Colour swatches shown are products from the PANTONE® Textile Colour System®. Reproduced under license. Pantone, Inc. trademarks are the property of Pantone, Inc. © Pantone, Inc. 2006. Produced under the permission of Pantone, Inc.

48 | Source | 2/2006 | © ontario

Perhaps inspired by Darwin's bicentenary in 2009 or by an interest in nature and the environment, this consumer's look expresses the spirit of the times.

Rain forest colors are interpreted here into a workable palette that will appeal to consumers.

MARKET SEGMENTS, BRANDS, AND COLOR CYCLES

Although many color forecasters may draw on the same social, cultural, and economic trends and so be likely to share some key influences, each forecaster will utilize inspiration and intuition to create a seasonal palette with individual interpretation and flair, providing color options for a variety of client and products.

BRAND IDENTITY

Color forecasters and their immediate clients—brands and retailers—have also come to realize that different **market segments** respond to different colors, and that a strong **brand identity** requires a unique color story that fits within the overall seasonal direction. The experienced color forecaster will not only investigate the cultural macro trends, but must also understand the needs of the individual brand or retail client. Color trends should be differentiated by market segment, brand identity, and price point.

On the other hand, price point can itself influence how colors will be used. New or offbeat colors are more likely to be utilized for avant-garde designer apparel, fast fashion, or accessories. Moderately priced clothing relies on colors that have already sold well at retail, or classics such as black, navy, or gray.

Market segment and price point are part of what defines a brand, but there is much more to brand identity. Brand identity has been described as a brand's "DNA" or "soul." Uche Nworah, a brand scholar and teacher at London Metropolitan University, describes a brand's DNA as "its Distinctiveness, Novelty and Attributes, as compared with those of the competition." Consumers are familiar with brands in all areas of product, and may be loyal to one brand or another because it suits their lifestyle—their age, interests, culture, and economic status.

If we look at a random list of consumer brands—Anthropologie, Lacoste, Calvin Klein, Liz Claiborne, Kookaï, Miss Sixty, Topshop, Timberland, Guess, Huit, All Saints, Prada, Hugo Boss, John Smedley—we can see that they have distinct brand identities and price points, along with color palettes targeting their core customer base. For example, Liz Claiborne's American-inspired classic colors appeal to a mid-market suburban customer, while Timberland's palette incorporates its customer's love of the outdoors. All Saints' line is grounded in black and offbeat darks, reflecting its edgy focus on the music business; and Prada's constant experimentation with color suits the designer-fashion loving consumer. Many brands are also retailers and sell their own make of clothing exclusively; for example, GAP, Next, J. Crew, Jigsaw, Mexx, River Island, Zara, and Mango.

Many department stores and large retailers also have their own brand identity, for example Bloomingdale's, Liberty, Harrods, Macy's, John Lewis, La Rinascente, or Bon Marché. If we were to describe their brand identities, Macy's and Harrods are identified by their claim to size and assortment; for many, Bloomingdale's is all about New York style, while John Lewis is tastefully British;

Within a market segment, such as students and young adults, there are many separate style tribes with different wants and needs.

Market segments are groups of customers with similar lifestyles, economic status, and shared interests, such as young families with children.

Hermès uses a signature color — orange — to make its brand identity clear, consistent, and easily communicated to the customer.

Liberty, La Rinascente, and Le Bon Marche are better known for well-edited quirkiness.

Many department stores and larger retailers now develop their own **private label** lines to appeal to their wider range of customers. Think of Per Una, Autograph, and Limited Collection at Marks & Spencer, or of Mossimo, Xhilaration, and C9 at Target.

Brand identity may include a signature use of color (Louboutin red, Juicy Couture pink, Eddie Bauer green, and Hilfiger's tricolor red, white, and blue) as well as utilizing color forecasting for its seasonal product.

For example, a brand such as Jigsaw is identified with soft, rich, often heathered or mélange colors in the key color families each season. If the color forecaster believes strongly in purple, camel, and pine green in a particular season, rather than in berry, taupe, and teal, the consulting forecaster will translate the key colors from the seasonal palette into the quieter, more complex versions preferred by the Jigsaw customer.

Another example might be a younger, trendier line for board sports. The brand would be identified with the colors of streetwear, certain rock bands, and social networking. Starting from the general seasonal palette, the color forecaster would make some colors brighter, some murkier, adding darks to create offbeat harmonies that would be quite different from the colors developed in the Jigsaw example, yet related to the overall seasonal message.

COLOR CYCLES

Color is also cyclical in nature, and the color forecaster will reference previous and current color palettes in the development of a new one. (Chapter 4 will examine color **cycles** in more detail.) Pat Tunsky tells us, "When developing a new season's color story I always have my last season's color palette at hand." And color consultant Anna Starmer, whose clients include Marks & Spencer and Monsoon, confirms, "If you have no knowledge of what is currently in the market, what has been successful or disastrous, then it is difficult to put together an accurate forecast for the future."

The application of a seasonal color forecast to suit individual product requires a thorough understanding of market segments, brand identities, and current color cycles in order to develop and offer a broad variety of fashionable color options to the customer each season, a process we will examine in more detail in Chapter 5. Like Robyn Waters' trendmaster, color forecasters "start out by observing a trend, but then they translate that trend information into a direction that makes sense for their companies and their customers."

Many department stores have a strong brand identity and may develop their own private label lines to appeal to their customer demographic.

Brands such as Toast are also retailers and sell their own make of clothing exclusively.

A seasonal palette developed for a younger brand such as Atmosphere would be quite different from one at GAP or Jaeger.

COLOR FORECASTING AND THE SUPPLY CHAIN

The interdependent nature of fashion and its related manufacturing industries, along with the complex and time-consuming nature of the **supply chain** today, means that color forecasting is an economic necessity. Global sourcing and fast fashion have compressed the timeline for product development, and the timely selection and accurate communication of color in the process are critical.

In addition to designers, product development teams, garment manufacturers, and retailers, color forecasters also advise fiber and chemical companies, yarn spinners, knitters and weavers, piece dyers, print studios, and manufacturers of findings (buttons, zippers, trims, thread, etc.).

Although the supply chain is an extremely complex subject, a quick explanation will help us understand where color forecasting fits into the process and why it is so important. There are a number of different sourcing scenarios utilized in product development, depending on whether the seller is a manufacturer, brand, or retailer; and on whether the seller is developing locally, or sourcing product as a fully made package, or contracting a factory to develop product to the seller's specifications (see timeline, pp.32–33). Technically complex apparel, such as activewear, intimate apparel, and swimwear, is often developed over a two-year time span; while knitwear and fast fashion can be developed more quickly, especially through local sourcing.

Fabric samples are usually produced in small dye lots (50–100 yards/45–90 m), while production dye lots can be thousands of yards. While in the past suppliers might have developed their own range of sample colors for the season, this is not economically feasible for the large competitive mills. All of the fabrics involved, as well as the findings for the garments, must be color-matched and approved to the designer's standards. Mistakes in color management not only cost in terms of materials but can result in late deliveries, which may require express shipments or lead to cancellations.

Many garment samples will be made up but may not make it into the final line. Designers may change their mind about the colors, or retail buyers may select some colors but not others. Because the process of dyeing sample lots and components is expensive and time-consuming, the design team must be confident in their selections and the direction provided by the color forecasters.

The supply chain for apparel is complex, and the production of fabric in appropriate colors depends on good color forecasting and communication.

Spinners develop and dye yarns some 18 months before the season, and the yarn fairs take place 12–15 months ahead.

Brands and retailers shop the textile trade shows 12 months in advance of the season.

Fabric mills and component suppliers use their color laboratories to match colors submitted by the brands and retailers.

Fabric samples are produced in small lots, while production dye lots may be thousands of yards long.

Fabrics and findings must be color-matched and approved to the designer's standards.

COLOR FORECASTING FOR LOCAL MARKETS

Finally, small local brands and knitwear manufacturers will often utilize the yarns and fabrics already dyed by their local suppliers, as the minimum dye lots required by many modern overseas dyehouses are prohibitively large, sometimes 10,000 yd (9,000 m) or more per color. The suppliers of better fashion fabrics, yarns, and findings, primarily in Europe, also consult with color forecasters about a year in advance in order to have the appropriate colors available for sampling and for small production orders.

Independent weavers, knitwear, and print studios will also look to color forecasting so that their patterns will reflect the colors of the season, and their suppliers of printing inks and dyed yarns will be prepared.

These suppliers may, in fact, produce their own color cards from sample lots so that color formulas are already developed. Fabrics, garments, and end products can then be locally produced and ready for market in a very short time, six months or less. For this reason, fast-fashion brands such as Zara (Inditex), Mango, H&M, and American Apparel are turning more to local sourcing.

The manner in which color is communicated along the supply chain is critical, and an understanding of the science and language of color makes the process of color matching and approval easier and more precise. We will examine these topics further in Chapter 3.

When we consider the complexity of the sourcing chain and the number of suppliers and manufacturers involved in bringing product to market, we can understand that, economically, color forecasting is essential. Brands, manufacturers, and retailers must limit the amount of product they develop, produce, and ultimately ship. Calling out the correct colors from the beginning eliminates waste, saves time, and encourages profitable results for all along the supply chain.

Independent weavers, knitwear and print studios also utilize color forecasting products and services so that their products will reflect current color preferences.

The local suppliers of better fashion yarns and fabrics may develop their own sample or stock lines based on the color forecaster's advice.

These collections by local designers and crafters benefit from an understanding of color trends and preferences.

THE ROLE OF COLOR FORECASTING IN THE SUPPLY CHAIN

Fabric is the single greatest cost in apparel production, up to 60 percent of the garment's "FOB" price (free-on-board, the price of finished goods cleared for export and loaded on the shipping vessel).

Color forecasters may contribute to trend concertations (committees) of textile shows such as Première Vision, advising participating mills for sample dyeing, and developing color cards for the show

Mills develop fabrics and may dye sample colors if making color cards or participating in textile trade shows

Brands begin fabric research and collect swatches

Retailers begin concept development for own product

Color forecasters continue to monitor designer, retail, consumer, and street trends and alert clients to new developments

Retailer lines send development packages to factories; suppliers dip colors for approval and produce sample lots for prototypes

Brands make up prototype garments

24–18 MONTHS BEFORE THE SEASON

Color forecasting organizations such as Intercolor and Color Marketing Group begin process of developing seasonal palette some two years ahead of season

Color forecasters and trend bureaux begin consulting with spinners, mills, and brands 24–18 months before the season. Retail product development groups follow shortly

Spinners develop yarns

Brands begin concept development

15 MONTHS BEFORE THE SEASON

12 MONTHS BEFORE THE SEASON

Color forecasters consult with retail buying teams and merchandisers

Yarn spinners, mills, and dye and chemical companies must have color-correct materials in place for textile shows and sample orders

Brands and retailers shop the textile trade shows

Brands order fabrics for prototypes and send development packages to factories

Retail fabric teams research and collect swatches

Mills and component suppliers begin to match customer colors; after approval, produce sample lots (50–100 yd/46–91m) for prototypes

10 MONTHS BEFORE THE SEASON

8 MONTHS BEFORE THE SEASON

Brand prototypes approved and "salesmen samples" made up in full color range

Retailer lines make up prototype garments. (While brands must develop a full line of salesmen samples to present to retail buyers, retailers' own lines have a more compressed timeline and can choose colors when production orders are placed)

Designer collections may influence colors or assortments to be chosen by retail buyers

Color forecasters may meet with brands and retailers to confirm colors before production orders and assortments are placed

Because they source and manufacture locally or regionally and control logistics, fast-fashion brands can wait for the designer collections six months ahead of the season before beginning much of their development

Brands present samples to retail buyers for ordering

Development teams for retailer lines review prototypes; meet with department buyers and merchandisers to choose colors and assortments

Brands, retailers, or manufacturers order production fabrics and trims. Color matching on production lots reconfirmed before garments manufactured

Fast-fashion retail brands work locally to develop colors, fabrics, and prototypes based on designer collections

Fast-fashion brands' production shipped, often utilizing their own logistics

6 MONTHS BEFORE THE SEASON

3 MONTHS BEFORE THE SEASON

4–5 WEEKS BEFORE THE SEASON

Garments inspected, packed, shipped, and delivered to brand or retail warehouse for distribution

Fast-fashion brands order production with local manufacturers; some may use own manufacturing facilities located near their distribution centers

CHAPTER 2
WHY AND HOW HAS
COLOR FORECASTING
EVOLVED?

THE DEVELOPMENT OF COLOR IN APPAREL

Color forecasting, as we know it today, is a modern discipline—the product of the Industrial Revolution and the subsequent creation of the ready-to-wear business. We have come to understand that color can have an emotional appeal for consumers through its identification with brands, cultural trends, market segments, and fashion tribes. In addition, we have seen that appropriate use of color in consumer products is an economic necessity, not only to drive sales, but to facilitate the product development process.

Through the centuries the deliberate and meaningful use of color has developed hand-in-hand with the growth of the textile and apparel trades, and is intricately linked with the development of dyestuffs. It was the evolution from handmade, bespoke clothing for the upper classes to factory-produced ready-to-wear for the masses that created the need for color forecasting as an integral part of the fashion industry.

EARLY TEXTILES

The human need to personalize one's appearance has always gone beyond merely covering the body, and the history of imparting color to fabric is nearly as ancient as the history of textiles. There are written records from 2600 BC regarding the use of dyestuffs in China; Roman graves from the second and third centuries AD contained madder- and indigo-dyed textiles.

Ancient textiles were completely natural, made primarily of wool and silk, along with linen and cotton. Dyestuffs were natural as well, including roots and treebark, animal urine, plants such as madder, saffron, weld, and woad, and insects such as lice and cochineal. Most colors were more subtle than those we see in the modern world, and were not particularly colorfast.

While early civilizations probably did not give much thought as to what color was fashionable, the scarcity and costs of certain dyestuffs made some shades more desirable. Purpura was a purple dyestuff made from the secretions of a particular Mediterranean mollusk; there is evidence of its use as far back as 1600 BC in Crete. During Roman times, purpura became so scarce that 1 lb (500 g) of purple cloth was worth $20,000 in contemporary terms.

In the early Middle Ages, dyers' guilds became established in Europe, and the art of dyeing was further influenced by textiles brought back from the Crusades and by the development of trade with Asia. Colors from China and Byzantium were brighter and dyestuffs were more evolved than those of early Europe.

The guild system was highly regulated and provided dyed fibers and fabrics primarily for royalty and the wealthy, as dyestuffs were very expensive. The vast majority of clothing, however, was worn in natural colors—the off-whites, blacks, browns, grays, and tans of the natural fibers themselves, or in home-dyed shades derived from local plants.

During the Renaissance the color of clothing became more important, indicating the wearer's cultural leanings, social hierarchy, and economic status. The silhouette, fabric, and color of one's apparel were indicative of personal status and class. Deep, rich colors were preferred by the nobility, the better to set off jewels and embroidery work.

Traders and courtiers traveling among the world's capitals returned with new and exotic styles in clothing and were in a sense the first fashion forecasters. By the seventeenth century a wide array of dyestuffs were traded around the world, and the increasingly consumer-based societies of Europe and the US drove the development of more and better quality colors.

Ancient textiles were dyed in infusions made from plants, insects, roots, and tree bark.

In the late fourth century AD purple dyestuffs were so expensive that Emperor Theodosium of Byzantium forbade the wearing of purple except by royalty; shown here on Empress Theodora.

Dyers' guilds were established in Europe during the early Middle Ages.

*During the Renaissance the growth
of a merchant class meant that
more people could afford a change
of clothes; colors indicated social
and economic status.*

THE INFLUENCE OF MECHANIZATION

With the invention of the mechanized weaving loom and industrial yarn-spinning machinery in the eighteenth century, silk and cotton fabrics became more readily available and affordable, and could be dyed in brighter colors than those achievable in everyday woolen fabrics.

The fashions of the French court of Versailles were brought back by visitors to Paris and were widely copied. Skilled dressmakers were employed by the wealthy, functioning as fashion forecasters on a one-to-one basis by advising clients on the latest fashions and assisting them in choosing fabrics and colors for their gowns.

By the beginning of the nineteenth century a wider array of fabrics became available, and fashion styles began to be promoted in women's periodicals through sketches and color plates. These, combined with the growing frequency of social gatherings, increased the public's awareness of fashion and color trends.

With Singer's mass production of the sewing machine in the 1850s, clothing could be made in factories, cheaper and faster than ever before. The nascent ready-to-wear business found a home in the newly established retail department stores, where the middle and working classes could purchase versions of the apparel worn by high society and portrayed in magazines.

Mass production of the sewing machine enabled the ready-to-wear business, and textile manufacturers began to demand dyestuffs with consistency and colorfastness.

SYNTHETIC DYES

As textile and apparel businesses expanded, manufacturers began to demand dyes with exact shades and colorfastness for lot-to-lot color matching. Dyers and chemists throughout Europe developed more concentrated dyes from traditional dyestuffs resulting in stronger, richer colors.

In 1856, one of these chemists, William Henry Perkin (see also p.100), accidentally discovered the first aniline dye, a purple called **mauveine**. Derived from coal tar, aniline dyes were the first truly synthetic dyes. The new color was greeted with enthusiasm by women from Queen Victoria and Empress Eugénie to the middle classes throughout Europe and America.

The invention of mauveine was followed by half a century of synthetic dye developments throughout Europe. Magenta, Hoffman's violet, scarlet, Bismarck brown, aniline black, methyl blue, malachite green, and synthetic madder and indigo all followed. These beautiful new colors were displayed to the public at a number of international exhibitions, including those in London in 1862 and in Paris in 1865, creating demand for these new and fashionable shades.

By the nineteenth century the upper classes were immersed in fashion, and early women's magazines increased awareness of color and fashion trends via color sketches and plates.

Allgemeine Woden-Zeitung,
Leipzig.

In 1856 William Henry Perkin
discovered mauveine, the first
truly synthetic dye. Mauveine
was an inexpensive version of
the previously unaffordable
purples worn by royalty and
the upper classes.

The new synthetic dyes were
brighter, less expensive, and
more reliable than natural dyes,
making beautiful textile colors
available to the mass market.

THE INFLUENCE OF THE FRENCH COUTURE

The latter part of the nineteenth century also saw a shift in the way fashion trends evolved. Working in Paris, Charles Worth established an atelier in 1858. By putting his name to his own designs and showing these clothes on live models in his salon, he changed the nature of fashion forecasting from a private relationship between dressmaker and client to the public expression of the designer's viewpoint.

In 1868 the first version of Le Chambre Syndicale de la **Haute Couture** Parisienne was established by Worth and his sons, primarily to copyright and protect their designs. During the remainder of the century, the couture grew in importance, confirming the fashion leadership of Paris.

In the late 1800s French textile mills began to issue color cards, swatched with paper or ribbon samples. These early color cards did not forecast color as much as show what colors were in vogue among the Paris dressmakers, and they had a great influence on the US ready-to-wear market. American manufacturers of fabrics, threads, leather, and millinery supplies began to match their dye lots to these Parisian shade cards.

At the turn of the century, new standards of wealth for the upper classes brought about the **Belle Epoque**, or "Gilded Age" as it was called in the US. Although more and more consumers were buying apparel off the rack, Paris was the epicenter of fashion inspiration. While it is difficult to establish dates for the first fashion shows, the Paris couture houses were showing their creations on live models in their salons as early as 1885. By 1913 designers were sending elite personal invitations to their clients to attend these shows.

By the end of the Belle Epoque the seasonal cycles of planning and developing fashion as we know them had fallen into place, with biannual fashion shows scheduled to suit the calendars of the society elite, as well as to cater to the increasing demand from professional buyers from the US. The couture showings were held in late January and late August. A select group of fashion consumers, US buyers, and editors were able to observe and disseminate the latest trends in silhouette, fabric, and color as decreed by the couturiers.

Working in Paris, Charles Worth was the first designer to attach his name to a line of his own creation.

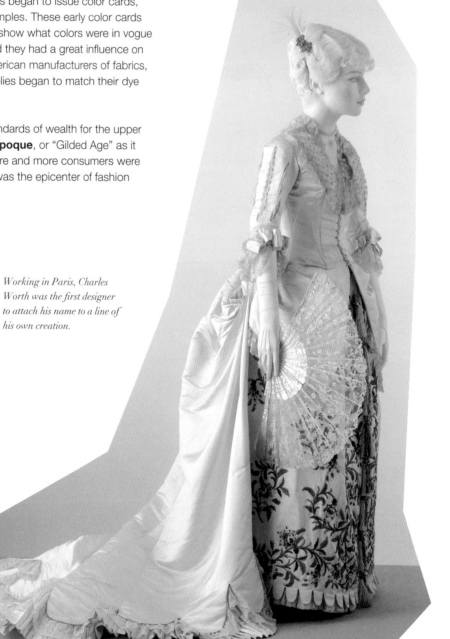

Color cards issued by French textile mills were popular with US manufacturers and retailers catering to a new mass market.

By the early 1900s, Parisian designers such as Paul Poiret (see also p.101) were changing the nature of fashion through their radical approach to color and design presented at seasonal couture shows.

DIEU! QU'IL FAIT FROID...
Manteau d'hiver de Paul Poiret

THE FIRST COLOR FORECASTING ASSOCIATIONS

As the ready-to-wear industry expanded in the US, garment makers and retailers began to visit Paris regularly, bringing back couture garments, fabric swatches, and color cards. Some even employed Parisians to observe and report on French style trends, setting the precedent for the fashion intelligence and marketing reports that continue to this day.

At this time, 90 percent of the dyes used by the US textile industry were produced in Germany, by giant chemical companies such as BASF and Bayer. With the advent of World War I, the US industry was cut off from both Parisian influence and German dyestuffs.

DEVELOPMENTS IN THE US

In the face of this disruption, the US textile mills, garment manufacturers, and related industries established a committee to develop a range of fashion colors for the next season that would utilize the dyestuffs available at home, and to have these colors dyed and issued as an American color card. In 1915 this group became the Textile Color Card Association, the first organization attempting to forecast and coordinate colors for an entire industry. This was a new approach, differing from the color cards provided by the textile mills that represented goods for sale or the colors selected by Parisian dressmakers.

After the war, US chemical companies exploited the patents of defeated Germany and developed an array of new dyes, pigments, and paints. The invention and commercialization of synthetic fibers, beginning with rayon in 1891 and followed by nylon in 1938, required new dyestuffs and methods of dyeing. Originally many yarn spinners and fabric mills issued seasonal palettes as selling tools, indicating the colors that could be achieved with the new fibers and fabrics.

During the 1920s color became a marketing tool in nearly every area of consumer product. "Color could make or break a retailer in the twenties, as the economic boom allowed more Americans to step through the portal of consumer society and buy ready-to-wear," writes American business author and consultant Regina Lee Blaszczyk.

The Textile Color Card Association was headed by a former actress and suffragist, Margaret Hayden Rorke—America's first professional color forecaster. Rorke made yearly shopping trips to Paris for the couture shows. She also collaborated with Bettina Bedwell, a *Chicago Tribune* fashion journalist, based in Paris. Bedwell tracked color trends and communicated them to Rorke, who matched the reports with her own forecasts. The New York fashion industry and its suppliers were enthralled, and the reputation of the Textile Color Card Association became well established. In 1955 it became the Color Association of the United States (CAUS).

Rorke and the association had set into motion a process of forecasting US color trends based on researching trends at the top of the fashion pyramid—Paris and the couture. While color direction now emerges from diverse sources around the world, Paris continues to exert its influence through its textile and trade shows, the seasonal designer collections, and the city's unique retail scene. Many international fashion designers call Paris home, and many color forecasters still consider a seasonal visit to Paris to be a cornerstone of their research.

In the years following, additional fashion and color trend associations were established, including some for profit. Founded in the US by Tobé Collier Davis in 1927, Tobe Associates was the first recognized paid fashion consultancy, and its weekly report was well respected as "the bible of the fashion industry." Using methods somewhat ahead of its time, The Tobe Report forecasted trends through analysis of consumer behavior and retail intelligence. Since 2005 the report has been part of New York's Doneger Group.

DEVELOPMENTS IN EUROPE

From 1931 through the 1960s the British Colour Council helped to forecast and set color standards for textile manufacturers and suppliers. In 1934 the BCC published its *Dictionary of Colour Standards* which defined color by hue, tone, and intensity (see Chapter 3), and was intended for the textile manufacturers and dyestuffs industry. The BCC definitions and its rather descriptive color names became the standards for many organizations in Britain, such as the Royal Horticultural Society, British Army, and Royal Mail.

But the onset of World War II intervened, and the fashion industry was put on hold for the next several years. After the war years of "making do," consumers emerged who were more educated and discerning, making up their own minds about fashion, and choosing clothing off the rack that was comfortable and practical. Meanwhile, in 1947 another for-profit forecasting service, Carlin International, was established, offering the French point of view.

In the post war boom, the influence of these new consumers on fashion and color trends would continue to grow, encouraging the development of areas such as **sportswear**, activewear, and career apparel. Fashion forecasting moved out of the hands of the Paris couture and became driven by more contemporary, popular, and commercial interests.

1917
FALL SEASON
Color Card of America
ISSUED BY
THE TEXTILE COLOR CARD ASSOCIATION
OF THE U.S.A., Inc.

MEMBERS OF THE TEXTILE COLOR CARD ASSOCIATION

SUNBEAM O. 4193 — BERYL O. 6154
TINSEL O. 4195 — DRAGONFLY O. 6156
SYRUP O. 4557 — TEAL DUCK O. 6567
VIRGIN O. 6193 — RASPBERRY S. 2165
MADONNA O. 6195 — CLARET S. 2167
TAPESTRY O. 6198 — BURGUNDY S. 2169
REDWOOD O. 2834 — PARTRIDGE O. 3924
MANZANITA O. 2836 — AUTUMN O. 3926
CHIPPENDALE O. 2838 — WALNUT O. 3929
LICHEN O. 5833 — BEGONIA O. 2033
PRIVET O. 5836 — SULTAN O. 2266

CINERARIA O. 2624 — CHRYSOPRASE O. 5152
CORONATION O. 2626 — ARSENATE O. 5154
WINE O. 2628 — SPEARMINT O. 5156
MIST S. 1803 — GLOXINIA O. 7584
STEEL S. 8065 — EMINENCE O. 7095
SMOKE S. 8935 — HORTENSIA O. 7588

FUR COLORS

POLAR BEAR O. 1048 — BEAVERPELT O. 8454
CHINCHILLA S. 8115 — CASTOR S. 8843
MOLE O. 8955 — KOLINSKY O. 4629
MOLESKIN O. 8957 — HUDSON SEAL O. 3949

The Textile Color Card Association was established in 1915 to provide the US industry with a range of colors utilizing the dyestuffs available in the US when European dyestuffs were cut off by WWI. In 1955 its name became the Color Association of the United States (CAUS).

In the post war era American women demanded a more practical, modern dress code, challenging the industry to develop color forecasting that was relevant to ready-to-wear and the mass market.

READY-TO-WEAR AND FIBER MANUFACTURERS' INFLUENCE ON COLOR

During the 1930s Parisian couture had grown increasingly outrageous and out of touch with the lives of women, who had become more independent and inclined toward a casual, more practical mode of dress. During the 1930s and 1940s, US sportswear emerged as a separate and successful fashion direction. Designers, including women such as Claire McCardell, Vera Maxwell, and later Anne Klein and Bonnie Cashin, established a rational, modern dress code composed of separates, career clothing, pants, and activewear.

"Fashion in America was logical and answerable to the will of the women who wore it. American fashion addressed a democracy, whereas traditional Paris-based fashion was authoritarian and imposed on women, willing or not," writes Richard Martin of the Metropolitan Museum of Art's Costume Institute.

This democratic attitude pointed the way to today's customer-centric fashion business, based on understanding the mind of the consumer. There was a definite need for trend and color forecasting that was relevant to ready-to-wear and the mass market, and the challenge was taken up by the emerging synthetic fiber business—fiber associations and newly powerful textile mills whose growth after the war was driven by pent-up consumer demand.

The invention of acrylic and polyester in the 1950s, along with new techniques in yarn spinning and texturizing, inspired a galaxy of new, branded fibers and fabrics. These were marketed to the buying public in a number of ways, such as garment hang tags and print advertising. They included registered names such as Orlon, Acrilan, and Creslan acrylic; Terylene, Crimplene, Dacron, Kodel, Trevira, and Fortrel polyester; and Antron and Ban-Lon nylon. Chief among these fiber companies was DuPont (now Invista) whose portfolio of fiber brands such as Dacron, Orlon, Tactel, Coolmax, and Lycra® continues to this day.

Fiber companies such as DuPont marketed their new branded synthetics (here, Dacron® polyester) through advertisements as well as through seasonal color cards.

While fiber companies marketed to the consumers to educate them and create demand, it was the yarn and textile companies who actually purchased the raw materials. Trevira® polyester is a global brand owned by Trevira GmbH.

MARKETING THE NEW FABRICS AND FIBERS

The giant chemical companies who made and sold the textile fibers—ICI, DuPont, Hoechst, Monsanto, Celanese, Lenzing, Enka, BASF, Rhône-Poulenc, and SNIA Viscosa, to name a few—went about marketing their products to the trade in a number of ways, including using seasonal color cards. These cards were generally developed by an in-house "fashion coordinator" or "fashion merchandiser" and featured swatches or reelings made from the branded fiber.

Several of the major fabric manufacturers—knitters and weavers—also invested heavily in marketing their products to garment manufacturers and retailers, as well as to the general public. Milliken, Burlington Industries, J.P. Stevens, Viyella, Courtaulds, Boussac, and others issued seasonal color cards, which involved the expense and effort of dyeing up sample lots of fabric. After assembling the color cards, excess fabric would be available for garment manufacturers to buy in small yardages for garment samples.

Not to be outdone, the suppliers of natural fibers, such as cotton, wool, and linen, formed their own marketing organizations. The International Wool Secretariat (Wool Bureau in the US) was founded in 1937 and became truly international in the late 1940s. In 1964 the Woolmark label was established; the company is now known as Australian Wool Innovation, owner of the Woolmark brand. It is jointly funded by Australian wool growers and the Australian government.

Lenzing, the Austrian company that produces Modal® and TENCEL® cellulosic fibers, continues to produce a beautiful color trend card each season.

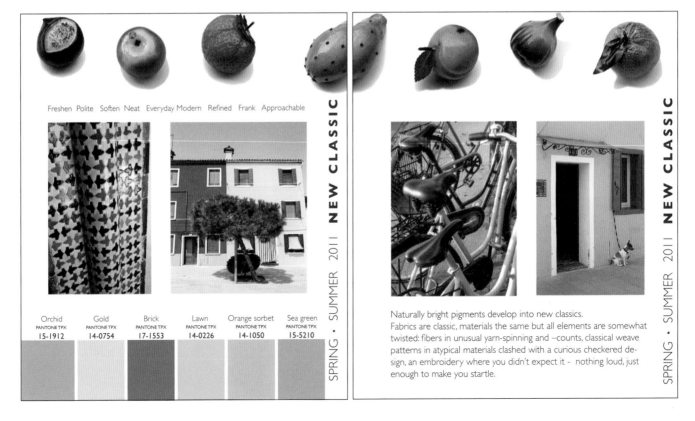

Freshen Polite Soften Neat Everyday Modern Refined Frank Approachable

Orchid	Gold	Brick	Lawn	Orange sorbet	Sea green
PANTONE TPX	PANTONE TPX	PANTONE TPX	PANTONE TPX	PANTONE TPX	PANTONE TPX
15-1912	14-0754	17-1553	14-0226	14-1050	15-5210

SPRING • SUMMER 2011 **NEW CLASSIC**

Naturally bright pigments develop into new classics.
Fabrics are classic, materials the same but all elements are somewhat twisted: fibers in unusual yarn-spinning and –counts, classical weave patterns in atypical materials clashed with a curious checkered design, an embroidery where you didn't expect it - nothing loud, just enough to make you startle.

SPRING • SUMMER 2011 **NEW CLASSIC**

Masters of Linen, a subsidiary of the European Flax and Hemp Confederation, was founded some 40 years ago. Cotton Incorporated, funded by the US cotton growers, was created in 1970 "to combat loss of market share due to consumers' infatuation with synthetic fibers." Each of these groups still produces fashion and color reports and forecasts in some form, shared through their websites, attendance at textile trade shows, and direct relationships with designers, textile manufacturers, and retailers.

The Cotton Incorporated color card and trend presentation is particularly well received. According to a company director, the cotton team is "the only American company invited to what's known as the early color committee meetings, which take place in Paris after the Première Vision fabric show. This gives us access to ideas from a select group who are considered among the most important color visionaries in the world."

The idea of branding a fiber or fabric by assigning it a trade name along with a set of marketable characteristics was a new concept for the fashion industry, and fiber or fabric brands became closely linked with the fashion services they provided. While these companies typically presented their trend information to the trade free of charge, marketing costs were ultimately recouped in product sales.

The fashion coordinators or fashion directors employed by the companies were responsible for developing the seasonal color palettes, as well as for consulting with and making presentations to the garment manufacturers and retailers. The costs involved with the development and production of the color cards were enormous, so it was important that the colors be saleable. Many

of today's leading trend and color forecasters honed their skills at fiber, yarn, and fabric companies such as DuPont, Monsanto, Dixie Yarns, and Courtaulds.

Since the 1970s the globalization of the sourcing chain has seen a shift to manufacturing of fabrics and garments at giant low-cost mills, primarily in Asia. Fabric mills and fiber companies in the West have been decimated, and those that have survived have eliminated in-house fashion forecasting. At the same time, brands and retailers have grown more powerful and established their own trend forecasting departments. At present only a few of the remaining textile companies in the West have the budget to develop their own palettes, while the majority of the giant Asian fiber companies and fabric mills lack the expertise and take color direction from their customers.

In 2011 there remain only a few fiber companies who still produce color forecast cards; these include Lenzing (cellulosics), Nilit (nylon), and Cotton Incorporated. With the exception of some of the specialized high-end European mills, fabric manufacturers no longer invest in seasonal swatch cards. This change contributed to the success of independent trend and color forecasting companies in the 1970s.

Masters of Linen's "Linstallation," amidst a field of flax in the Paris Palais Royal during the 2010 couture week, which promoted linen using new concepts in color and design.

ΦHASE OUT

Candlelit 11-0617 TCX	
Yolk 15-1157 TCX	
Flushed 16-1329 TCX	
Lady Slipper 19-2030 TCX	
Porcelain 12-1206 TCX	
Lukewarm 14-4206 TCX	
Black Raspberry 19-2524 TCX	

Home

Maddar Dye 17-1547 TCX	
Gypsum 13-1209 TCX	
Cracked Amber 16-1346 TCX	
Newsprint 19-1314 TCX	

There is a collective yawn at watching rebellion without reason, simply for the sake of getting noticed. No longer interested in the pointless provocation of shock tactics, 'quick fix' anything and risqué art form, people demand real genius. This psychoanalytical look at pop culture reveals that it still pops, it's also ushering in skill and thoughtful endeavor because true magnificence need not be broadcast.

Colors are opulent but untypical. No jewel tones but sultry plays of deep Lady Slipper and Black Raspberry become lighthearted alongside pale shades of Flushed, Candlelit and Porcelain. The faded blue is a silent strong color, important for the season and Yolk is the pop that invigorates the combination.

Today Cotton Incorporated continues to produce well-respected color and trend reports for the trade, along with an advertising campaign that keeps cotton products uppermost in consumers' and manufacturers' minds.

THE FASHION PRESS ENTER FORECASTING

Since the eighteenth century, women's magazines have played an important role as fashion advisors. Color sketches reproduced through lithographic printing brought the latest trends from Paris and other capitals directly to the consumer. With the proliferation of fashion photography in the early twentieth century, a new type of journalism—the fashion magazine—made this information more widely available. Magazines such as *Vogue* and *Harper's Bazaar* not only disseminated fashion information, but through their editorial choices influenced the success or failure of many designers and trends.

While fashion editors are viewed primarily as reporters, the most powerful among them—such as Diana Vreeland at *Vogue*, Carmel Snow and later Liz Tilberis at *Harper's Bazaar*, and Carrie Donovan at *The New York Times Magazine*—have forecasted and promoted fashion and color trends as well through their influence within the design community. In 2011 editors such as Anna Wintour and Emmanuelle Alt at the US and French editions of *Vogue* continue in this tradition.

Fashion coverage from the daily newspapers has given us influential editors such as Suzy Menkes at the *International Herald Tribune*, Sarah Mower and Hilary Alexander at *The Daily Telegraph*, Cathy Horan and Amy Spindler at *The New York Times*, Colin McDowell of *The Sunday Times Style Magazine*, and Robin Givhan of *The Washington Post*.

The powerful magazine editors were once in a position to assist the fiber and fabric manufacturers with placements at the popular fashion houses. The manufacturers sold goods and placed hang tags; the apparel manufacturers saw their creations featured in the editorial pages of prestigious magazines; the magazines received more ad revenue.

FABRIC EDITORS AND DEPARTMENTS

To further this success story, the leading magazines created fabric departments with fabric editors who researched the markets, attended the textile trade shows, and created color and fabric trend presentations to share with the trade. Here, then, was another form of color forecasting. *Vogue, Harper's Bazaar, Mademoiselle*, and *Glamour* magazines all had fabric libraries which displayed the latest European (and American) fabric offerings. Their fabric editors would meet one-on-one with the designers of the day to advise on color and fabric direction for the next year.

But as textile and apparel production shifted to lower-cost producers in Asia, and Western fabric and fiber companies were consequently forced out of business, the magazines no longer had the benefit of their ad revenues. By the 1990s the fabric editors and their departments were gone. While the fashion magazines no longer sport fabric editors or fabric libraries, the fashion press remains intrinsic to the reporting and development of trends.

TRENDSETTING

Trade magazines and industry newspapers have also had an influence on the development of seasonal trends. *American Fabrics* was a trade publication founded by publisher and graphics artist William Segal in 1946 and edited for many years by his French wife, Marielle Bancou-Segal. It was known as "the *Fortune* magazine of the textiles and garment industry." The full-color, swatched magazine was published into the 1970s and remaining editions have become collectors' items.

The View publications, headed by David Shah in Amsterdam, are a range of magazines well known since 1988 for thoughtful forecasting and evocative imagery. Editors of some of these influential magazines include trend forecasters Martin Raymond and Li Edelkoort, of *Viewpoint* and *Bloom* respectively.

Drapers in the UK and *Women's Wear Daily* in the US remain powerful, daily newspapers with an online presence dedicated to the apparel trade. Their fashion and fabric editors not only report the trends, but can influence a design's success with their reviews. Today these publications focus on retail and business news, consumer analysis, and the runways.

Trade magazines such as View, *edited by some of the most respected color and trend forecasters of the day, influence the development of seasonal trends.*

Benefiting from the advertisements placed by the textile and fiber companies, the leading fashion magazines established fabric departments with editors who created color and fabric presentations and consulted with designers to advise them of upcoming trends.

RUNWAYS AND THE DISSEMINATION OF COLOR

Fashion shows were once another way in which the fashion designer communicated directly with the customer. During the early years of the couture, fashion editors were invited to the shows but were allowed only to sketch, as photographers were not welcome. The scope and setting of the runways changed after World War II as the fashion industry emerged from its period of hibernation into "The Golden Age of Couture."

The cultural upheavals of the 1960s resulted in radical changes for the fashion industry. In Paris, young designers such as Yves Saint Laurent, Pierre Cardin, and André Courrèges broke with the Chambre Syndicale (the organization that controls Paris fashion). London's "young designer" movement included Mary Quant, Ossie Clark and Celia Birtwell, Barbara Hulanicki of Biba, and Zandra Rhodes, among others.

The opening up of the market to younger, inexpensive fashion was an opportunity for the powerful fiber and textile companies, such as Courtaulds and ICI, who backed the growth of young fashion with design contests, cooperative advertising featuring their creations, and their own design shows. As **prêt-à-porter**, or the ready-to-wear, business began to eclipse the couture, the runways evolved into the semiannual Fashion Week showings of today. Since the 1970s the major Fashion Weeks—New York, London, Paris, and Milan—are staged six months ahead of the selling season. They are closely watched by all elements of the trade, as well as by fashionistas everywhere, for directions in silhouette, color, and fabric, and for color trends in accessories and beauty.

They are also reviewed at length by fashion editors of magazines, major newspapers, trade press, and Internet sites. Their commentary can help popularize the trends shown on the runway; or have the opposite effect.

While the fast-fashion segment is able to take advantage of runway trends, today's color forecaster must be savvy enough to look beyond Fashion Week's confirmation of the current season, and pick up hints of newness for development of next year's colors and trends. Today's color and fashion forecasting begins much earlier in the cycle and is based on many factors beyond the runways.

Early fashion shows were very genteel, but in 1947 Christian Dior's "New Look" revitalized the Paris couture. French designers began to understand the marketing power of the fashion show.

In London, Mary Quant was a key figure among a group of young and independent boutique fashion designers who epitomized the fall of elitist fashion.

During the 1960s the fashion industry changed with the times, and the young Parisian designers such as Yves Saint Laurent and André Courrèges established ready-to-wear collections targeting the younger market.

Today the runways of the semiannual Fashion Weeks are mined for inspiration by designers, retailers, the press, and consumers around the world.

TREND SERVICES AND THE TEXTILE TRADE SHOWS

While stock fabric houses and showrooms for boutique designers were the norm in London, Paris, and New York into the 1960s and 1970s, longer lead times and lower costs were necessary for democratized, mass-market fashion. Much of this fashion was still inspired by the designs shown in Paris, and the translation of a particular garment into mass production and distribution could easily take a year. The large fiber and fabric companies who were driving the industry at that time required major commitments of raw materials and could not change direction quickly.

During the 1960s the European community established a number of fiber, fashion, and trade fairs to bring a sense of order to the development process. Although these trade shows were ostensibly about selling goods, they became venues for researching the color and fabric trends for the next season.

Interstoff, the first fabric fair, began in 1959 in Frankfurt, and quickly became an important venue for gathering trend information as well as for sampling and ordering fabric. In 1973 a group of fabric manufacturers from Lyon organized Première Vision (PV) in Paris, specifically to show the seasonal color and fabric trends of the French mills before the Salon du Prêt à Porter.

Held in February and September, PV is attended by textile and apparel designers, sourcing managers, retail product development teams, and of course by color forecasters from around the globe. While the exhibitors' booths are closely guarded, the color and fabric trend displays provided by the show are considered by many to be a must-see. Many apparel and retail organizations that may not place orders at PV send representatives to shop the trends.

PV has expanded considerably since its inception, moving to its current location at Paris' Parc des Expositions in 1983, and has gradually opened up to select exhibitors from other countries. In Florence, Pitti Filati, the yarn and knitwear exhibition, started up in 1977 and was also recognized for its color and trend forecasting function.

Timing has always been an issue for the fabric fairs and, as they have grown, the calendar has been pushed forward. In the 1950s, couture showings highlighted the trends some three weeks *after* the beginning of the selling season; in the 1970s, Interstoff began forecasting the trends eight months *before*. This change meant that spinners, textile manufacturers, designers, and retailers were better able to synchronize trends across the industry.

Since the 1970s additional trade shows have been added to the international fashion calendar, with lead times extended to several months ahead of the selling season (see Major Apparel Textile Trade Shows calendar, p.61). We now have Expofil, a fiber and yarn show integrated with PV; Interfilière, a fabric show for intimate apparel and swimwear; Texworld, a mass-market fabric show positioned to compete with the more upscale PV; Milan's Milano Unica, combining Ideabiella, Ideacomo, Moda In, Prato Expo, and Shirt Avenue; and several textile shows in Asia, including the giant Intertextile Shanghai. There are additional textile shows throughout Asia, Europe, the US, and Latin America.

According to Pascaline Wilhelm, Fashion Director for Première Vision, color forecasting for the trade show is accomplished by a primarily European committee made up of producers and

The Première Vision trade show presents colors and fabrics a year in advance of the season.

COULEURS
INTERFILIÈRE A/H 2010-11
INTERFILIÈRE COLOURS A/W 2010-11

Gamme Couleurs Eurovet avec l'aide de spécialistes de la lingerie /Eurovet Colour Range with the assistance of lingerie specialists : Comité Français de la Couleur Mélody Mizraki & Gaëlle Evorah, **Concepts Paris** Jos Berry & Jennifer Kell, **Nelly Rodi** Nicole Tottereau, **Promostyl** Sophie Laffite, **Stijlinstituut amsterdam** Anne Marie Commandeur, Agnès d'Anselme, Florence Peyrichou, Véronique Moriez, Invités de la saison / Guests of the season: **Eurojersey** Nello Marelli, **Bureau de style Le Bon Marché** Nicole Bernardo

Interfilière is a trade show featuring fabrics for intimate apparel and swimwear; colors may relate to global trends but will be specialized for the market.

The color forecast at Première Vision is developed by a concertation (committee) of experts 18 months in advance of the season. Exhibiting mills are required to dye sample yardages to reflect the colors determined by the committee.

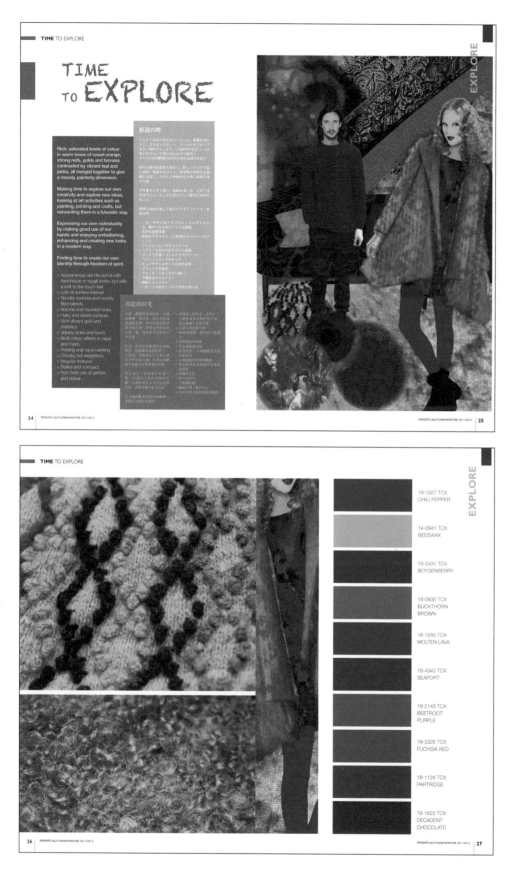

The yarn fair SpinExpo, held in
New York and Shanghai, is also
recognized for its color and trend
forecasting function, along with
Pitti Filati in Florence.

promoters of fibers and yarns, promotional groups and fashion organizations, associations of stylists and trend bureaux, and international salon representatives. This gives the trends at PV a sense of authority, allowing designers to view and sample fabric in the recommended colors of the new season.

Beyond the fabric fairs, the democratization of fashion has also resulted in the proliferation of independent committees of industry experts and paid trend bureaux, providing color and trend forecasting, retail analysis, and marketing concepts.

While the fiber and fabric companies exerted a great deal of influence over color trends in the 1960s and 1970s, their color cards often conflicted with one another. There was a need for independent forecasting groups that were not focused on selling fiber, yarn, or fabric. Intercolor, the International Commission for Fashion and Textile Colors, was launched in Paris in 1963. It is a nonprofit organization, funded by membership fees.

In Europe most of the countries that export fashion have similar nonprofit associations or groups to brainstorm and develop color trends. These include the British Textile Colour Group, the Deutsches Mode Institut, and Comité Français de la Couleur.

Color Marketing Group, another nonprofit association, was established in 1967 in the US. These committees convene twice a year, some *two years* ahead of the selling season (see also Chapter 5).

Also in 1963, an innovation in color matching technology was introduced by a company called Pantone to sell a standardized book of colors and home furnishings; the company now issues seasonal color forecasts for the fashion industries through their PANTONE® FASHION + HOME Color System.

SCOTDIC is a provider of color references organized according to the Munsell color system (see p.74). Introduced in 1982, the company does not forecast color, but is used to match color by many designers, manufacturers, and retailers. We will look at color systems and color matching in more detail in Chapter 3.

Originally established as a color standards service for the graphic arts, Pantone is now a global supplier of color standards for the apparel and home furnishings market in cotton and paper formats as well as providing seasonal color forecasts through the PANTONE® FASHION + HOME Color System.

The British Textile Colour Group, like Intercolor and Color Marketing Group, is an independent forecasting group that is not focused on selling fiber, yarn, or fabric.

SCOTDIC is a well-known provider of standardized color references; the company does not forecast color.

COLOR FORECASTING TODAY

Color forecasting today is undertaken by a spectrum of organizations. The International Colour Authority was organized in 1966 by a group of publishers from Amsterdam, London, and New York, including William Segal, founder and publisher of *American Fabrics* magazine. Currently owned by William Benjamin, the ICA forecasts color two years ahead of time; the palettes are available by subscription. The private trend service Promostyl began selling its forecasts on color trends, lifestyle, and buying preferences in 1967.

Other commercial trend bureaux include Trend Union (Li Edelkoort), Peclers Paris, LA Colors from Amsterdam (Lousmijn van den Akker), Doneger Creative Services (Pat Tunsky), d.cipher fm (Christine Foden), NellyRodi in Paris, Concepts Paris by Jos Berry (specializing in trends for intimate apparel), A+A Design Studio *(Andrea Dall'Olio)* in Milan, SCOUT in Australia, Fordecasting, Huepoint, Mudpie (juniors, kids, denim, and activewear), as well as publications such as the PANTONE® VIEW Colour Planner.

While each of the above has its own format, these color forecasts share similarities in their composition and presentation. The colors are most often represented in yarn or fabric of natural materials (unless the provider happens to be a synthetic fiber company); some services provide paper tabs or numbered references from Pantone, SCOTDIC, CAUS, the British Colour Council, or another recognized catalog of color standards.

Designers, brands, and retailers now have many options for color forecasting. They may purchase or subscribe to the services of various trend bureaux such as Promostyl, Peclers Paris, or Carlin International; or might be active members of a membership committee such as Color Marketing Group or the British Textile Colour Group. Color forecast displays at the trade shows are free, but organizations such as Première Vision charge for the physical color cards.

The "rat race of design innovation" has become "increasingly intensified and frenzied over the years," says Shinobu Majima, Associate Researcher at the University of Manchester. Communication, commerce, and travel have become accessible to a wider audience, fostering cross-fertilization of cultural and fashion trends at an ever-faster speed.

The advent of the Internet has radically altered color forecasting and trend development in the twenty-first century. Blogs and websites allow immediate access to color direction generated from designers, trade shows, trend services, and global culture. While some are free, there are many by-subscription Internet fashion services too, including WGSN (Worth Global Style Network), Stylesight, TrendPulse, Trendstop, Trendzine, and Fashion Snoops. Web-based services such as WGSN (launched in 1998) and Stylesight (from 2003) offer real-time consumer research and trend analysis, along with reporting on trade shows and the retail business.

In addition to fiber companies, trade shows, and professional organizations, color forecasting today is undertaken by numerous commercial trend bureaux and publications such as the PANTONE® VIEW Colour Planner.

'Imagine...'

PANTONE® VIEW COLOUR PLANNER WINTER 2009/10

WOMENSWEAR • MENSWEAR • ACTIVEWEAR • COSMETICS • INTERIORS • INDUSTRY • GRAPHICS

PANTONE® VIEW Colour Planner's seasonal forecasts are organized into themed palettes with inspirational graphics and a written color story.

SEA PINK

LEMON DROP

OCEAN WAVE

MAGENTA PURPLE

BLITHE

EVERGREEN

BRIGHT VIOLET

CLEMATIS BLUE

Imagine ... and dream

Let your dreams come true!
Don't be afraid to express yourself...

Spontaneous sophistication in a totally eccentric universe.
Haute culture inspiration, exuberant but extremely curious.
Strong character can seduce without clichés.
Brave tones go away from boring ambients.
New luxury connected to modernity and differentiation.
Be free!

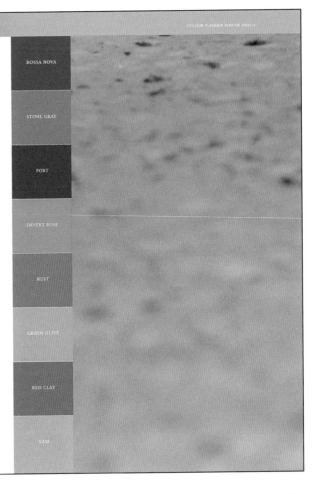

BOSSA NOVA

STONE GRAY

PORT

DESERT ROSE

RUST

GREEN OLIVE

RED CLAY

YAM

Imagine ... the planet

The planet feeds the imagination. The evening sky turns red and ochre yellow. Shadows traverse the cocoa earth. Lush green dims in bitter gloom. Winter gains the heart and melancholy fingers strum a tune. Colours recede and beckon the imagination to follow. Imagination heals the heart with promises or memories of spring. Deep in the universe a planet is spinning. These colours are the smiles planted deep in the cold earth.

While color forecasting is primarily directed at the trade, Internet access allows consumers to preview color and fashion trends in real time. Savvy brands and retailers utilize Facebook, YouTube, and Twitter to communicate directly with their customers to ascertain their wants and needs. The PANTONE® FASHION + HOME Color System has recently begun marketing to the consumer through homewares, fashion accessories, and wedding planning. The whole process of forecasting colors for apparel has been thrown into overdrive, with consumer input becoming a key driver for product development.

Since the 1960s, many color and fashion trend services have come and gone, including Nigel French, IM International, Jenkins UK, Design Intelligence, Index, Color Portfolio, Color Incorporated, and Li Edelkoort's View on Color. The recession of 2008/2009 saw an increasing number of insolvencies and redundancies as more fashion companies cut spending on consultants and brought trend development in-house.

Today color forecasting is evolving away from the concept of "one trend fits all" and returning to more specialized trend stories. Most brands and retailers now develop proprietary color palettes for their target customer, based on their own information gathering, plus paid one-on-one consultations with independent color forecasters or with consulting members of the for-profit trend services. The use of multiple sources of information, including customer surveys, blogs, websites, and social networking sites, has become increasingly vital to the development of color stories appropriate to a unique retail or brand identity.

There is no doubt that color forecasting is a critical part of the fashion business and will continue to evolve to keep pace with the changes in retailing, marketing, and the use of new media in the twenty-first century. "Fashion today is a global enterprise, which exhibits a most powerful system of trend creation that other commodity markets, such as automobiles and electronics, have keenly followed," observes Majima.

Commercial trend bureaux such as Peclers Paris are based in fashion capitals around the world.

While the PANTONE® FASHION + HOME Color System is directed primarily toward the trade, Pantone® has taken its brand directly to the consumer through a number of collaborations with brands such as Uniqlo.

MAJOR APPAREL TEXTILE TRADE SHOWS

Exact dates change yearly, but this chart indicates seasonal timing. (Additional textile shows in the US have formerly been held in New York, Las Vegas, Los Angeles, and Miami Beach but have not had meaningful long-term success and were discontinued.)

EVENT	SEGMENT	TIMING PRE-SEASON	CALENDAR DATES
Première Vision Color Concertation (Paris)	Color	18 months	September, February
Yarn Expo Shanghai	Fibers and yarns	18 months	March, August
Expofil (Paris)	Fibers and yarns	18 months	Concurrent with PV
SpinExpo (Shanghai)	Fibres and yarns for knitwear	18 months	March, September
PV Preview (New York)/Direction by Indigo	Fabric and pattern design	13 months	January, July
Texworld (New York)	Fabric	13 months	January, July
Printsource (New York)	Pattern design	13 months	January, April, August
SpinExpo (New York)	Fibres and yarns for knitwear	13 months	July
Intermoda (Guadalajara, Mexico)	Fabric	13 months	January, July
Tissu Premier (Lille)	Fabric and textile technologies	13 months	January, September
Interfilière (Paris) (1)	Fabric and trim for intimate apparel	13 months	January, July
Colombiatex (Medallin)	Fabric and sourcing	13 months	January
Pitti Filati (Florence)	Yarns for knitwear	13 months	January, July
Première Vision Pluriel (Paris) (2)	Fabric, trims, print studios, leather	12 months	February, September
Texworld (Paris)	Fabric	12 months	February, September
Milano Unica (3)	Fabric	12 months	February, September
Text Styles India (New Delhi)	Fabric, fiber, and yarn	12 months	February
LA International Textile Show	Fabric, and trims	11 months	March, September
Interstoff Asia (Hong Kong)	Fabric	11 months	March, October
Intertextile Beijing	Fabric (Spring)	10 months	March
Yarn Expo Beijing	Fibers and yarns	16 months	Concurrent with Intertextile
Intertextile Shanghai	Fabric (Fall)	11 months	October
Fashion Week (4)	Apparel for Fall	5 months	February
Fashion Week (4)	Apparel for Spring	4 months	September

(1) Interfilière Evolution Days are held in Paris two months ahead of the main fair. The organization also holds fairs in Hong Kong and Shanghai. **(2)** Première Vision Pluriel includes Expofil, Mod'Amont, Indigo, Le Cuir, and Zoom. PV also holds shows in São Paulo and Moscow. **(3)** Milano Unica combines Ideabiella, Ideacomo, Moda In, Prato Expo, and Shirt Avenue. **(4)** The International Fashion Week shows take place in New York, London, Milan, and Paris.

THE DEVELOPMENT OF COLOR FORECASTING

Color forecasting for fashion emerged through the centuries as the design, manufacturing, and sales of textiles and apparel changed with the industrial revolution and the social, economic and technical developments affecting civilization.

Trade with East brings new colors and dyes

The Crusades

Florence becomes known for dyeing

Medieval dyers guilds established

Marie Antoinette and court of Versailles inspire fashion

Royalty, the court, and their dressmakers set fashion trends

Color forecasting evolves with Industrial Revolution and transformation from handmade to mass-produced apparel

Silk and cotton become less expensive; brighter colors can be used

"Gilded Age" of Art Nouveau, Expressionism, Ballet Russes, Orientalism

Paul Poiret brings bright color and lifestyle concepts to fashion

Paris salons establish regular show schedule, issuing invitations to clients, buyers, and press

French fashion mined for inspiration by US industry

Advent of photography launches fashion journalism

4TH CENTURY

Use of natural dyestuffs until 1856: plants, bark, roots, animal urine

Scarcity of certain dyes creates color hierarchy

Byzantium emperor Theodosium decrees purple as royal

Purpura purple dye made from mollusks (*genus Murex*)

12TH–13TH CENTURY

14TH–16TH CENTURY

Clothing color represents social and economic status; courtiers bring new styles from travels

The Renaissance and rise of merchant class; exploration, trade, travel

Dark colors preferred by courtiers to set off jewels

Most of population wears natural or undyed wool

17TH–18TH CENTURY

19TH CENTURY

Singer sewing machine launches ready-to-wear industry

Willliam Perkin and invention of synthetic dyes 1856

Growth of department stores

Charles Worth establishes first couture house; influence of Parisian fashion

Beginnings of Paris couture 1868

French textile mills issue color cards, inspiring US manufacturers

BELLE EPOQUE (1874–1914)

First fabric fair, Interstoff, established 1959; independent forecasting services boom through 1960s

Mass-market fashion takes off with new synthetic fibers and fabrics

Fiber and fabric companies issue color forecasts, driving fashion marketing

1960s youth culture inspires designer rebellions in London and Paris, where Saint Laurent leads break from the Chambre Syndicale

Fashion press and editors influence trends in fashion, color, and fabrics

Color forecasting available from paid consultancies, industry organizations, and trade shows

Brands and retailers drive proprietary fashion and color development

Development of fashion blogs, social networking, and Internet fashion services increase pace of change

Internet provides real-time fashion information to all

THE WORLD WARS

POST WORLD WAR II

1970s–1990s

21ST CENTURY

US cut off from German dyes during WWI

Textile Color Card Association founded 1915; Tobe Report first paid consultancy 1927

US chemical companies develop new dyes, paints, and synthetic fibers

Roaring 1920s stylish flappers; color becomes a marketing tool

Emergence of US sportswear; fashion becomes democratic and customer-centric

Globalization of textile/ apparel industries

Apparel production moves East, advancing the forecasting calendar

Western textile companies decline

Color forecasting becomes two-year cycle

Textile trade shows expand globally, providing forecasting information

Semiannual Fashion Weeks established

Influence of street fashion

CHAPTER 3
THE LANGUAGE
OF COLOR

COMMUNICATING IN COLOR

The color forecaster is the first link in the establishment and communication of color direction and color standards for apparel and fashion-related products. Because the perception and understanding of color are subjective, however, it is critical that we use a standardized language.

Over the years a scientific understanding and means of communicating color has developed, along with classification systems that enable us to communicate and match color standards, create harmonious color palettes, and successfully produce and market the right color to the customer.

The scientific language of color is rooted in color theory, and familiarity with this vocabulary will assist the color forecaster in communicating with accuracy. Color theory is a combination of physics, art, and psychology.

The communication of color involves color forecasters, designers, lab technicians, dyers, chemists, and product development managers working across the globe and using a variety of languages, light sources, and materials. "Ineffective communication, especially on color, has severe ramifications in terms of time, cost, quality and overall profitability to today's apparel retailers," according to Glen Littlewood in *Total Color Management in Textiles*. (Formerly with Datacolor, in 2011 Littlewood is Sales and Marketing Director of VeriVide; both are suppliers of **color management systems**.)

Even when using standardized terms such as **hue**, **value**, **chroma**, and **color temperature**, though, the communication of color is affected by our personal perceptions, the source of light, and a number of other factors.

Bauhaus color and design teacher Josef Albers wrote in Interaction of Color, *"In visual perception, a color is almost never seen as it really is—as it physically is."*

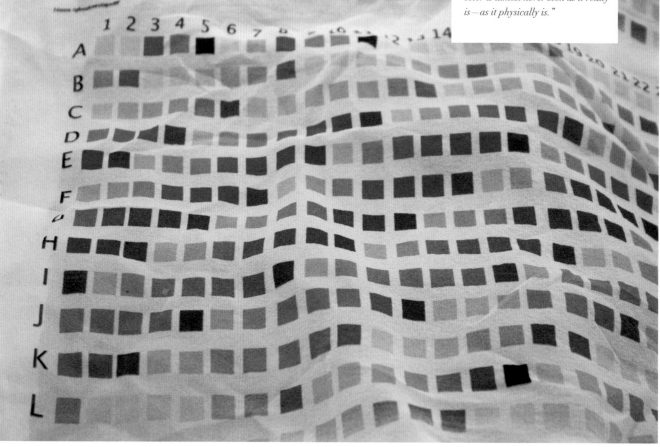

The four components of color that enable us to understand and communicate what we see are hue, value (luminance), chroma, and temperature:

*Hue is the term for the pure spectral colors we know by their color names: red, orange, yellow, green, blue, indigo, and violet. The color **spectrum** is the band or series of colors ordered in accordance with the magnitude of their wavelengths, as discovered by Isaac Newton (see p.70). Colors that can be produced by the visible light of a single wavelength are referred to as the pure spectral colors, and every color can be defined by some combination of wavelengths. A rainbow comprises the pure spectral colors or hues we know by the names red, orange, yellow, green, blue, indigo, and violet.*

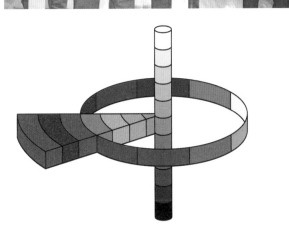

*Value tells us how light or dark a hue is, relative to white. Value is the relative lightness or darkness of a color; a color with a high amount of white has a high value, or luminance, while a color closer to black has a lower value. For example, bright yellow would have a higher value than navy blue. A **shade** is a hue with the addition of black, while a **tint** is produced by the addition of white, as in these gradations of blue. White, black, and gray are known as the **achromatics**—they are without hue.*

*Chroma measures the strength or purity of color (absence of gray), and is similar to **saturation** or intensity, which relate to the paler or stronger appearance of a hue under different lighting. The addition of gray to a hue creates a **tone**. Hues differ in their chroma; some hues, such as red, are more powerful than others. All hues do not reach their maximum chroma strength at the same value. For example, the strongest yellow hue is by nature much lighter, or higher in value, than the strongest blue hue.*

Colors are said to have cool temperatures (green, blue, and violet), which are relaxing, or warm temperatures (red, orange, and yellow), which are stimulating. "Undertone" is the primary hue that defines the temperature of a color. Yellow and violet can be considered either warm or cool, depending on the undertone. Achromatics (black, white, and gray) can also appear cool or warm.

PERCEPTIONS OF COLOR

Bauhaus color and design teacher Josef Albers (see also p.75) stated in his *Interaction of Color* that, "If one says 'Red' (the name of a color) and there are 50 people listening, it can be expected that there will be 50 reds in their minds. And one can be sure that all these reds will be very different." In everyday conversation we communicate color via descriptive names such as grassy green, sky blue, or lemon yellow, and are likely to describe the intensity of a color as light, pale, deep, or bright. More sophisticated users of color may even describe them as dusty, fluorescent, atonal, warm, or cool.

PHYSICAL FACTORS

We have already seen in Chapter 1 that individual interpretation of a color is influenced by its cultural and psychological meanings. Our perceptions are affected by any number of external and internal physical factors as well. It is estimated that some 7 percent of males and 0.4 percent of females are color-blind to some extent, according to the Howard Hughes Medical Institute; and studies have shown that yellowed vision becomes prominent over the age of 75. The **light source** is also a prime consideration. While daylight is often considered a pure source of light, it can change with the position of the sun in the sky, by its northern or southern orientation, and with altitude, cloud cover, or atmospheric pollution. Indoors, fluorescent lighting will cast cooler light (an absence of red), while incandescent lighting appears warm (an absence of blue), according to the General Electric Company.

The influence of varying light sources needs to be very carefully considered when matching **color standards**. Have you ever purchased two items of clothing that matched in the store, but did not match outside in daylight? **Metamerism** is the term for colors that match under one light source, but do not match under another. Neutrals can be especially difficult to match accurately.

A color standard is the exact color desired for a product that has been agreed upon by the necessary decision makers, and referenced via some standardized color matching system or measuring system so that everyone in the supply chain is working with the same data and materials. Designers sometimes submit colors on paper, plastic, paint chips, or other **substrates** to be matched in textiles at the very beginning of the process.

Color will read differently on a reflective surface than on a matte surface, and textile fibers and structures absorb dyestuffs at different rates. Color on fibers with a high luster, such as silk and some synthetics, will seem more intense or fully saturated than the same color in wool or a matte fiber; and it can be difficult to achieve some colors on certain fibers (see also p.154). The use of a single textile color standard for a project is critical to the success of color communication.

In addition, a color's surroundings alter the brain's interpretation of the color. For example, a gray circle will appeal lighter against a black background than against white; and a green circle against a blue background will seem yellower than a green circle against a yellow background, which will read as bluer. This is known as **simultaneous contrast**, or **Chevreul's Law**, first propsed by Michel-Eugène Chevreul in 1839 (see also p.73): "Two adjacent colors, when seen by the eye, will appear as dissimilar as possible." This phenomenon must be kept in mind when matching a solid color to an area in a high-contrast printed pattern, for example.

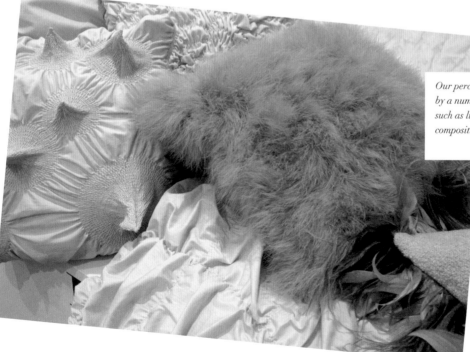

Our perception of color is affected by a number of physical factors such as light source, and a product's composition and surface texture.

The casual communication of color relies on our internal memory of the natural world, as in "lemon yellow."

We may use inaccurate words such as light, pale, deep, or bright to describe the intensity of the color blue.

COLOR NAMES

To add to our confusion, the commercial use of color as a marketing tool relies on descriptive names to promote a particular ambience, mood, or brand identity. A designer's color palette for a particular season may be inspired by the seaside, resulting in color names such as pink sand, seafoam, tidal pool, or seashell. These names may mean one thing to the designer, but something different to the fabric dyer, or retail buyer, ad photographer, or ultimate consumer.

The use of mail-order catalogs and Internet shopping has encouraged the development of very unique color names. A Fall 2009 listing of cashmere sweaters by American retailer J. Crew included colors such as bright coral, heather latte, bright hydrangea, light berry, cinnamon spice, and burnished olive. On UK retailer Boden's website, cardigans were offered in crocus, dark turquoise, fennel, fuchsia, periwinkle, ultramarine, and zest. Although these color names are poetic and appealing, they can also be confusing to the less sophisticated shopper. In addition, colors shown on websites and in catalogs may not accurately depict a product's true color.

"Even when we disregard the vagaries brought on by color vision, the identification of colors is confusing in its subjectivity," writes Sarah Lowengard in *The Creation of Color in Eighteenth-Century Europe.* "Names differ by language, region, producer, preparation methods, and occasionally the whim of a merchant."

COLOR AS LIGHT: UNDERSTANDING ADDITIVE COLOR

When he wrote that, "Colors are the children of light" in his 1963 book, *The Art of Color*, artist and Bauhaus teacher Johannes Itten gave poetic expression to the basic understanding of color first developed by Isaac Newton. In 1672 Newton refracted white light with a prism, creating what he called the "spectrum" of color visible to the human eye: red, orange, yellow, green, blue, indigo, and violet—or as we know it, the rainbow. *Spectrum* is Latin for "appearance" or "apparition."

Newton also showed that the prism was not creating color by refracting the colors back through a second prism into white light, demonstrating that light alone is responsible for color, and that adding together the colors of light results in white.

At the beginning of the nineteenth century, scientists such as Thomas Young, Hermann von Helmholtz, and James Maxwell developed explanations of color vision known together as the **tristimulus theory** of color perception. These scientists came to understand that light is made up of energy vibrations of differing wavelengths, each representing one of the **pure spectral colors**. Light is a type of electromagnetic wave; the colors we perceive depend on the wavelength of the light we are seeing.

Objects themselves do not have color, but we perceive the color of the light reflected from them. An object is perceived as a particular hue because that wavelength is being bounced back, while all the other wavelengths are being absorbed—a red flower appears red because the wavelength we perceive as red is reflected.

The range of wavelengths the human eye can perceive is called "visible light." The human eye receives the light waves through millions of rods and cones in the retina, which convey shades of gray and color hues to the brain respectively. There are three types of cones, which differ in their color sensitivity: to red-orange, green, and blue-violet. Thus, the human eye is capable of seeing the three **primary colors of light**—red, green, and blue—and

can be fooled into seeing the full range of visible colors through the proportionate adjustment of these three. These are not the same as the primary colors of artists' pigments or subtractive color (see below); they relate directly to the color reception of the cones in the eye and the wavelengths we are capable of perceiving.

The simultaneous projection of the three primaries of light results in white light, just as in Newton's refraction of the rainbow back into white light (**additive color theory**). This can be visualized as the white light seen when three primary colored spotlights overlap on a wall.

Two primaries of light can be mixed to form a **secondary color of light**. Red + blue gives us magenta, green + blue yields cyan, and red + green creates yellow. When one of these secondary colors is mixed in the proper proportion with its opposing primary—the color *not* used to create the secondary color in question—the result, again, will be white light. This means that any primary color of light is a **complementary color** to the secondary one created by mixing the other two primaries.

However, most art and design work utilizes paints, pigments, or ink for fabric, paper, or canvas. As colors are added to a white ground, light is subtracted or absorbed; the results get darker and move toward black. Think of adding layer upon layer of paint or crayon onto paper; eventually all the white light is subtracted, and the absence of light is black. This is known as subtractive color.

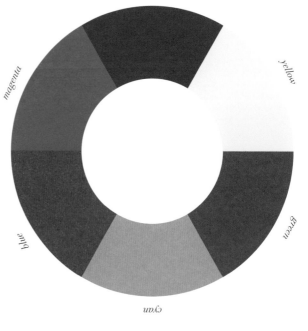

Light wheel

The primary colors of light—red, green, and blue—correlate to the wavelengths perceived by the cones of the human eye; adding these colors together creates white.

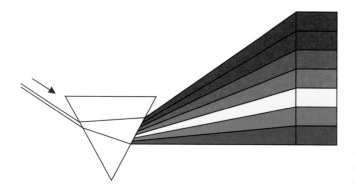

In 1672 Isaac Newton refracted white light through a prism, demonstrating the spectrum of color visible to the human eye.

COLOR AS PIGMENT: UNDERSTANDING SUBTRACTIVE COLOR

Subtractive color utilizes a set of primary colors that are different from the colors of light and forms the basis of most contemporary color theory. During the eighteenth century, scientists continued to investigate Newton's ideas about color. Artists, dyers, and printers knew the principles of mixing color empirically, and believed that red, yellow, and blue (RYB) were theoretically capable of mixing all other colors. In **subtractive color theory**, primary colors are defined as those hues that exist naturally and cannot be created by mixing other colors.

The **primary colors** of paints, pigments, and dyestuffs, then, are red, yellow, and blue (RYB); these are slightly different hues than the primary colors of light (red, green, and blue; RGB). In subtractive color theory, the combination of the primary colors of pigments—red, yellow, and blue—will move toward black, subtracting out the light.

In additive color, the absence of color (light) is black. In subtractive color, the summation of color is black.

COLOR AND PRINT

Contemporary color management is further complicated by the differences between digital media, using the measurement of light or additive color, and printing that utilizes subtractive color. The RGB colors we see on the computer screen are created with light using the additive color method. As more color is added, the result is lighter and moves toward white.

Printing, however, is based on subtractive color theory and a different set of primary colors. As color photography evolved early in the twentieth century, three-color printing became economically feasible in mass media, and the theory of color for printing was adapted to the primary colors of cyan, magenta, and yellow (CMY)—the same as the secondary colors of light.

The **printing primaries** (CMY) are defined as absorbing only one of the retinal primary colors. Remember that each secondary color of light (here defined as the printing primaries of CMY), combined with its opposing or complementary primary, creates white. As each printing primary (CMY) is layered by the printer, the primary colors of light (RGB) are absorbed, and the result moves toward black. Therefore, printed color is subtractive. Current printing processes utilize a separate black ink in addition to CMY for a richer black (CMYK).

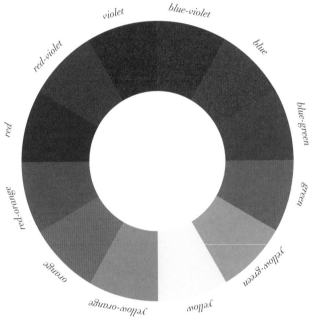

Pigment wheel

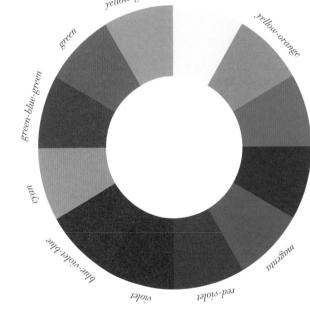

Process wheel

The primary colors of paints, pigments, and dyestuffs are red, yellow, and blue; the combination of these colors moves toward black.

The printing primaries cyan, magenta, and yellow absorb the retinal colors of red, green, and blue; as each printing primary (CMY) is layered by the printer, the primary colors of light (RGB) are absorbed, and the result moves toward black.

EARLY COLOR THEORY AND THE EVOLUTION OF THE COLOR WHEEL

Isaac Newton divided his refraction of light into seven colors named in their order: red, orange, yellow, green, blue, indigo, and violet. He chose seven colors based on an ancient Greek belief that there was a connection between the colors, the musical notes, the known objects in the solar system, and the days of the week! We now know that this arrangement is due to the individual wavelength of each color: we perceive the light with the longest wavelengths as red, and the light with the shortest wavelengths as violet.

Using the seven identifiable colors of the spectrum, Newton created the first color wheel. The physical format of a circle offered information about color relationships, demonstrating the complementary pairings of red with green, yellow with violet, and blue with orange.

GOETHE AND COLOR PERCEPTION

The first person to explore the physiological effects of color was the German poet and scientist Johann Wolfgang von Goethe. In his 1810 *Theory of Colors*, Goethe explained that the sensations of color reaching the brain are shaped not only by the physics of light, but by the mechanics of human vision and by the way our brains process information.

Goethe also believed that the temperature of color alters how it is perceived and its psychological effects. This is possibly because warm hues generally have a higher chroma (intensity) and value (luminance) compared to cool hues. Goethe divided all the colors into two groups: the plus side (warm) including red, orange, and yellow, and the minus side (cool) including green, blue, and violet.

Goethe also drew attention to the simultaneous contrast of colors. A red against a violet will appear more yellow, while the same red against orange will appear more blue. In other words, the temperature of a color will appear warmer or cooler depending upon the colors surrounding it. In the same way, a color will have a brighter effect on a dark background, and vice versa.

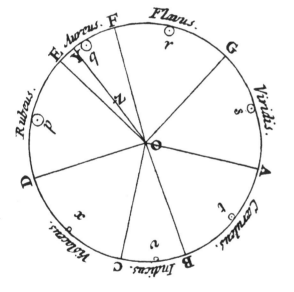

Isaac Newton shaped the seven colors of the visible spectrum into the first color circle, which became the model for many color systems and theories during the eighteenth century.

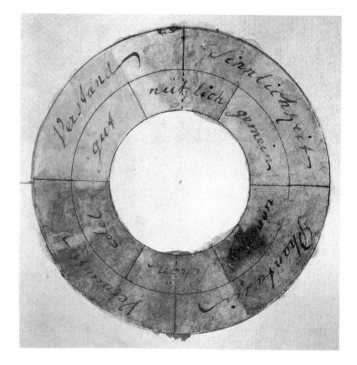

Goethe's color wheel explained complementary colors as "those which reciprocally evoke each other in the eye."

CHEVREUL'S EXPANDED COLOR WHEEL

Chemist and head dyemaster of the famous Gobelins tapestry works in Paris, Michel-Eugène Chevreul further defined the concept of simultaneous contrast. Chevreul developed his first "chromatic diagram" in 1855, and demonstrated that a color will lend its adjacent color a complementary tinge. For example, a swatch of yellow against a blue background will appear tinted orange, because orange is the complementary color to blue.

With these relationships in mind, Chevreul set out to organize colors for the manufacture of textiles in a new dimensional version of the color wheel. Using the subtractive primary colors of RYB, he added three **secondary colors** (orange, green, violet) and the six additional **tertiary colors** (created by the mixture of one primary color with one adjacent secondary color on the wheel). Each segment was then divided into six zones for a 72-segment circle.

Chevreul also demonstrated the effect of white or black on a hue by dividing each radius into 20 steps in order to specify brightness (value). With white at the center, each fully saturated hue could then be located on the radius within its segment according to its brightness. For example, pure yellow, with a higher value, would lie closer to the center than pure blue.

Chevreul organized colors for textiles in his color wheel, adding secondary and tertiary colors, and demonstrating the effect of value (black or white) on a hue.

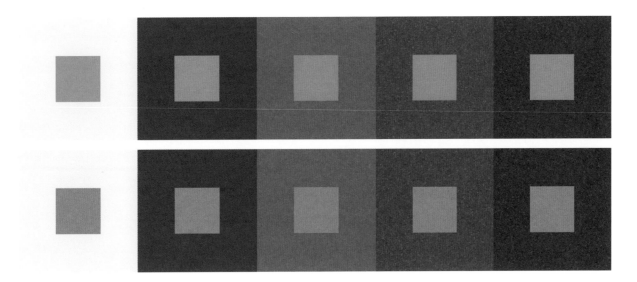

A color's surroundings will alter the brain's interpretation of the color, making two adjacent colors seem as dissimilar as possible. This is known as Chevreul's Law.

CONTEMPORARY COLOR THEORY: MUNSELL, ITTEN, AND ALBERS

While Chevreul successfully portrayed both hue and value in his color wheel, it did not depict the aspect of chroma, or the effect of gray on color tones. Various two-dimensional attempts using single and double pyramids, cones, cubes, and spheres were cumbersome or inaccurate in practical application.

As color wheels became more complex, the number of color variations grew geometrically. The naming of colors beyond the recognized 12 primary, secondary, and tertiary hues was more challenging when value and chroma were incorporated. The communication of color via color names became inadequate and, as we have seen, was open to interpretation due to cultural factors, lighting, setting, and so on.

MUNSELL'S ALPHANUMERIC SYSTEM

At the turn of the twentieth century, artist and professor Albert Munsell wanted to create a "rational way to describe color" that would use **alphanumeric** notation instead of color names, which he could use to teach his students. *A Color Notation* was published in 1905. It depicts colors on an irregular sphere, and each color was referenced with a designation such as 10RP 4/10, which correlated with its hue, value, and chroma.

Munsell begins with five "simple" hues of red, yellow, green, blue, and purple; and combines them to create five "compound" hues. The ten hues are represented on the sphere in longitudinal segments, each given an alphabetical notation, and each segment is subdivided into ten more sections.

Value is represented on a vertical axis with white at the top and black at the bottom. If this axis is considered as achromatic, chroma is measured from the center (gray, or without hue) toward the outside of the sphere (full saturation). Two colors of equal value and chroma, on opposite sides of a hue circle, are complementary colors, and mix additively to the neutral gray of the same value.

Munsell determined the spacing of colors along the dimensions by taking measurements of human visual responses. Because all colors do not reach their maximum chroma strength at the same level of value, Munsell's sphere would actually be quite bumpy rather than perfectly round. Each color is fully specified by listing the three alphanumerics for hue, value, and chroma. For example, the designation 10RP 4/10 would specify the color's hue as the tenth section of the red-purple hue, with a value of 4 and a chroma of 10.

Using his sphere, Munsell's concepts of color balance and harmony utilizing combinations of hue, value, and chroma are quite easy to understand, and provide sound concepts for creating workable color palettes. For example, he suggests combining complementary or opposing hues in equivalent or balanced chromas. When combining values of the same hue, he suggests that a low value/weak chroma of a hue will harmonize with a high value/strong chroma of the same hue.

The Munsell color system, with its alphanumeric notation, allows us to visualize the interplay between hue, value, and chroma. It inspired the development of standardized commercial systems such as Pantone and SCOTDIC, used today for color matching by forecasters, designers, and color labs.

ITTEN AND HARMONIC COLORS

However, it was Johannes Itten's color theory that, in the mid-twentieth century, changed the way color is understood. As part of the Bauhaus school of design in Germany, Itten was influenced by geometry and expressionism. He applied geometry to the color wheel developed by his teacher and contemporary painter, Adolf Hölzel, inventing a three-dimensional color star within the 12-hue color wheel, and seven principles of color contrast that utilize hue, value, and chroma to provide models for color schemes. Using his color wheel, Itten developed 26 different combinations of **harmonic colors**: sets of two or more colors in relationships that are pleasing to the eye.

In *The Art of Color* Itten wrote that, "Harmony implies balance, symmetry of forces" and taught that colors used in balance would produce gray when mixed together. He also believed that color has a spiritual and psychological effect, and that concepts of color harmony are very individual. He associated color palettes with personalities, designating them with the names of seasons, and inspiring our current concept of seasonal colors and palettes.

ALBERS AND THE PERCEPTION OF COLOR RELATIONSHIPS

Probably the most influential artist–educator in modern times was Josef Albers, who studied under Itten at the Bauhaus, then went on to replace him as teacher. While chairman of the Department of Design at Yale University he wrote *Interaction of Color,* first published in 1963. Albers' book investigated the effects of color relationships on our perceptions of intensity, temperature, transparency, vibrating and vanishing boundaries, and reversed grounds, which he had begun to explore in 1950 in a series of paintings entitled *Homage to the Square.*

In an interview for the Smithsonian Institution in 1968, Albers explained that his teachings were not about color theory, but about developing an "eye for color." "In my color book there is no new theory of color. But in it there is a way how to learn to see." He believed that no color theory on its own could develop one's sensitivity to color, but that through practical exercises and experience one could come to understand the physical relationships between colors, as well as their psychic effects.

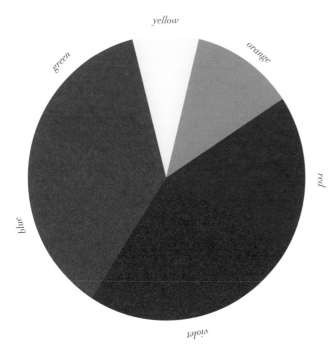

According to Itten's Contrast of Extension, different amounts of one color are needed to balance another. In this illustration, red and green balance at a ratio of 1:1, orange and blue at a ratio of 1:2, and yellow and violet at a ratio of 1:3.

BUILDING AND UNDERSTANDING THE SUBTRACTIVE COLOR WHEEL

The subtractive or artists' color wheel is a representation of the relationships between colors, and is a useful tool for understanding color contrast, harmony, and balance when developing a **color scheme**, or combination. The easiest way to understand the color wheel is to build one. The three primary colors of red, yellow, and blue are spaced around a 12-hue circle, so that they can be connected by an equilateral triangle.

The secondary colors are mixes of two primary colors. Red + yellow will yield orange, yellow + blue creates green, and blue + red gives us violet. These secondary colors are placed equidistant from their component colors on the color wheel, again so that they may be connected by an equilateral triangle.

The tertiary colors will fill in the six spaces left in the color wheel and each comprises one primary color and one adjacent secondary color on the wheel. This means that a tertiary color is 75 percent of one primary color, and 25 percent of a second primary color. These colors are red-violet, red-orange, yellow-orange, yellow-green, blue-green, and blue-violet.

This basic color wheel does not take value (luminance) into consideration and assumes that the primary colors have the highest possible chroma (intensity) to begin. The 12 places on the color wheel can be subdivided to create any number of colors, as Chevreul demonstrated in his 72-hue color wheel, and Munsell later expanded on.

Through the color wheel we can easily see the relationship of complementary colors directly opposite one another; for example, red and green, blue and orange, or yellow and violet. In subtractive color theory, the combining of complementary colors moves toward gray or a dark neutral. Complementary color schemes create a harmonious contrast, particularly those made up of the primary and secondary colors. In complementary pairs of tertiary colors there is an underlying color relationship, and the contrast is less strong. For example, the complementary tertiary pair yellow-green and red-violet have the primary color blue in common.

We can also see that half of the wheel is made up of warm colors, while the remaining half contains cool colors. Every hue has an undertone based on one of the primary colors, and it is this undertone of red or blue that determines its temperature. Yellow and violet are generally considered to be more temperate colors. It is possible for a cool hue, such as blue, to have a warm undertone, and vice versa. Likewise, the **undertone** of a secondary hue will take on the temperature of the undertones of its primary components. In other words, two primary colors with a warm undertone will create a secondary hue with a warm undertone, and vice versa. Mixing colors with different undertones will theoretically create a more temperate secondary color.

While the color wheel evolved through the centuries, Itten's 12-hue version is most used by today's color professionals, designers and students as a tool for understanding color relationships. By combining the 12 basic hues with one another, altering them through value (adding white or black) and chroma (adding gray) or by mixing them to create **neutrals**, we can visualize an infinite variety of colors to use in creating a palette.

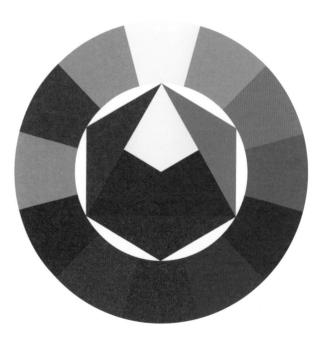

Based on the color theory of Bauhaus artist and teacher Johannes Itten, the most commonly used color wheel has 12 hues.

USING THE COLOR WHEEL TO BUILD COLOR SCHEMES

An understanding of the color wheel and the relationships between colors allows the color forecaster to transform seasonal color trends into a pleasing palette. While a retail season may have a dominant color family or hue, we now understand that colors do not stand alone, but are perceived in relationship with surrounding colors.

The color forecaster subconsciously applies certain principles of color theory to create harmonious combinations or schemes that will work on the retail sales floor as well as in the consumer's closet. This is what is meant when we say that the forecaster or designer "has an eye for color," as Albers described it. These principles are based on the relationships between the hues, or pure colors. Once these are understood, variations of value and chroma (the creation of tints, shades, and tones) can be employed to realize an infinite number of color combinations.

Using the above principles, most color combinations developed would be called "harmonious." Think back to Itten's concepts of harmony and balance—that colors used in balance would produce gray when mixed together. However, there are some color schemes that are **discordant**. This implies that they have broken with the natural order of color. For example, a hue with a high value such as yellow may be changed to a shade by the addition of black, and combined with tint of a hue with a naturally lower value, such as violet. This combination of yellow shade and paled violet would be considered discordant.

Another discordant combination is that of a hue and the color immediately to the right or left of its complement—the simultaneous contrast. Discordant color schemes are not necessarily undesirable, but may be used for particular effects. Adjusting the value of the hues is often used as a device to render discordant and clashing color combinations more pleasing.

Incorporating these principles may seem unnecessarily rigid and non-creative, but as they become second nature they will make building a workable palette much easier. Color theory and the color wheel are simply tools of the trade; they provide a common language through which color forecasters, designers, manufacturers, and retailers communicate. Take the time to examine color combinations, prints and patterns in fabrics, and apparel to identify and understand the following color schemes.

Neutrals are made up of multiple complementary colors and thus contain all three primary colors in varying proportions. They appear muddy or earthy since their component hues are not pure, and will have warm or cool undertones.

The monochromatic color scheme

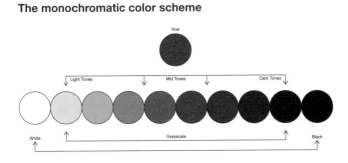

The monochromatic color scheme combines two or more colors that are shades, tints, or tones of the same hue. In other words, it is a group of colors derived from a single hue but varying in value and/or chroma.

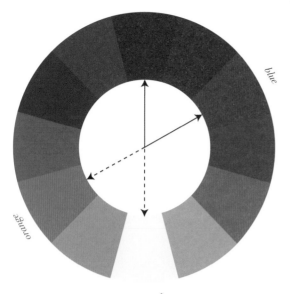

violet

blue

orange

yellow

The analogous color scheme

The analogous color scheme combines two or more colors that are adjacent or close to one another on the color wheel. The colors are linked by an underlying hue in common. For example, using Itten's 12-hue color wheel, all of the colors containing red could be used in an analogous color scheme, from red-orange to blue-violet.

These scarves present a clear example of a warm and cool analogous color scheme.

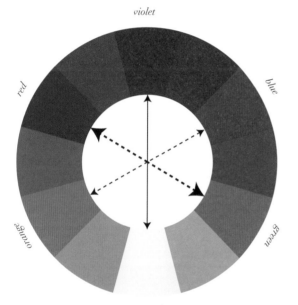

violet

red

blue

orange

green

yellow

The complementary color scheme

The complementary color scheme is the easiest to understand—the colors are opposite each other on the color wheel. These colors are harmonious through contrast, which is most pronounced between the six basic hues of red/green, blue/orange, and yellow/violet. On the 12-hue color wheel, other complementary combinations have an underlying color in common. Changing the value or chroma of these hues, of course, will create a variety of possible combinations.

The use of yellow and violet in this vintage scarf illustrates a complementary color scheme.

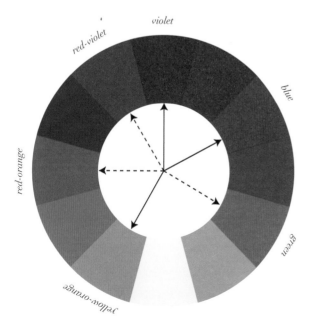

red-violet

violet

blue

red-orange

green

yellow-orange

The split complementary scheme

The split complementary scheme offers more nuances while maintaining contrast in the scheme. It uses a hue along with the two hues either side of its complementary color. For example, green would be combined with red-violet and red-orange, the two colors adjacent on the color wheel to green's complementary, red. Again, tints, values, and tones of the hues will create more interesting combinations.

Yellow-orange works in a split complementary scheme with violet and blue; here blue is not a pure hue but has been altered with gray to create a tone.

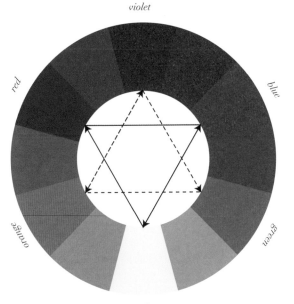

The triadic color scheme

The triadic color scheme (or harmonious triad) uses three colors equally spaced around the color wheel. This offers strong visual contrast but is not as contrasting as the complementary scheme. It is easiest to understand by using an equilateral triangle in the center of the color wheel. Adding black, white, or gray to the hues will provide more alternatives.

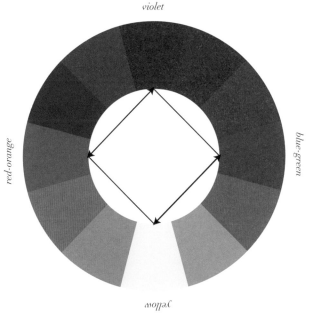

The tetradic color scheme

The tetradic color scheme may utilize double complementaries or double split complementaries. In the first combination, two sets of complementaries, such as violet/yellow and red-orange/blue-green, are joined by a square inside the color circle. This scheme can appear very complex to the eye if all four colors are used in equal amounts; it works best if one color dominates and the other hues have altered values.

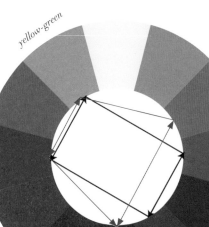

The double split complementary

In a double split complementary, the hues on either side of two complementary colors can be linked by a rectangle or trapezoid. For example, if the complementary colors chosen were red and green, the double split complementary possibilities would be red-violet and red-orange with blue-green and yellow-green (rectangle); or red-violet and red-orange with blue and yellow, or yellow-green and blue-green with violet and orange (trapezoid).

MANAGING COLOR COMMUNICATION

Once the color forecaster (or designer) has created a palette for the season, the colors—with all their nuances—must be communicated down the line to yarn and fabric dyers, printers, merchandisers, photographers, and visual display managers. While storyboards may be created with pieces of yarn, snips of paper, evocative photographs, and found objects, the proposed palette must be translated into color standards, or physical fabric swatches (lab dips). This is usually accomplished in one of two ways: colors in the palette can be matched to the closest reference in one of the color management systems such as Pantone or SCOTDIC; or the target (whatever is representing the desired color) may be mathematically measured; this is known as colorimetry.

THE COLORIMETER

During the early twentieth century a French organization, the Commission Internationale de L'Eclairage (International Commission on Illumination, or CIE), developed a model for graphing colors according to their wavelengths, matching them against the three primary colors of light perceived by the human eye: red, green, and blue. The system used a **colorimeter** to measure the three variables of color hue, luminance (value), and purity (chroma) in terms of human eye-brain perception.

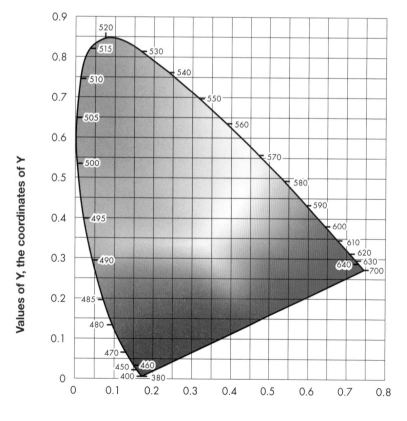

Values of X, the coordinates of X

The **tristimulus values** *(based on the tristimulus theory of color perception) are expressed as X, Y, and Z respectively on a* **chromaticity diagram**. **Chromaticity** *is the quality of a color as determined by its dominant wavelength and purity, or chroma. As standardized by the CIE, chromaticity is represented by X + Z, while the Y value represents the luminance, or value of the color. When these X and Y values are plotted on a chromaticity diagram, the spectral colors follow a horseshoe-shaped curve. All visible colors fall within the resulting closed curve. Further calculations on the graph can be used to determine the dominant wavelength of the color, or the target being measured.*

THE SPECTROPHOTOMETER

The **spectrophotometer** is a more powerful instrument, capable of spectral analysis of the wavelength transmitted by an object without human interpretation. Spectral data is the most complete and precise means of describing a color, by specifying the amount of each wavelength that the target reflects.

This form of color communication works well, but only if the data is accurate and reliable. Calibration of computer monitors and spectrophotometers can affect the outcome, as can metamerism (see p.68). It is critical that the equipment within a supply chain is calibrated to the same standards, and that technicians are fully trained.

Remember, too, that computer screens and monitors utilize additive color, while printing and textile pigments utilize subtractive color. The colors portrayed on the screen will not be exactly the same as the physical materials being matched.

Today most major brands and retailers utilize some kind of digital or electronic color communication tool, allowing them to match and share colors accurately within their supply chain, saving time and money.

COLOR ATLASES

While digital color technology will continue to evolve, outside the lab many color forecasters utilize a "color atlas" or management system designed specifically for textiles for visual communication of color standards. The best-known systems, SCOTDIC and Pantone, are used globally.

The SCOTDIC system is based on the Munsell color system (see p.74); the colors are dyed on cotton, polyester, or wool. It is probably the most extensive textile color system in the market, with some 2,300 colors available in cotton, 2,468 in polyester, and 1,100 dyed in wool. Starting as a kimono factory in Japan, SCOTDIC has been in business for 100 years. SCOTDIC also offers its own software systems for building palettes and communicating throughout the supply chain.

The SCOTDIC system of fashion colors uses Munsell numeration, with each color alphanumerically identified by its hue, value, and chroma.

Originally established as a color standards service for the graphic arts, today the PANTONE® FASHION + HOME Color System's 1,900-plus chromatically arranged colors are available on paper as well as on cotton.

Unlike SCOTDIC, the PANTONE® FASHION + HOME Color System is regularly updated via seasonal color forecasts. This can cause some confusion, as the numbering system is sequential and does not reflect the chromatic placement of the colors.

Pantone also offers spectral data (electronic files with the colorimetry for a specific color number) for those who require digital color confirmation, and has aggressively marketed its brand via digital integration with a number of design software systems and apps for the iPhone and iPod Touch.

Founded in 1979, Natural Color System, a Swedish color order and communication system for architecture, design, industry, and education, is growing in popularity among designers, but does not currently use textile materials in its products. Other color atlas systems include the *Munsell Book of Color*, the Inter-Society Color Council (ISCC), the British Colour Council's *Dictionary of Colour Standards,* Ridgway's *Color Standards* (a color system proposed by Roger Ridgway in 1912 for identifying the colors of flowers, insects, and birds), the Maerz and Paul *Dictionary of Color*, and the Plochere Color System. In addition to information, these reference books can provide inspiration when developing evocative color names for a seasonal palette.

Like many of the skills used in color forecasting, the language of color is both aesthetic and scientific. While textile and apparel designers will need a much deeper knowledge of the science of color, an understanding of the color wheel and color theory will provide the color forecaster with the necessary language to convey the artistic and aesthetic goals of a palette with balance, harmony, and most importantly, with accuracy.

The PANTONE® FASHION + HOME Color System uses two digits followed by a dash and then four digits and either a TPX (paper) suffix or a TCX (cotton) suffix. Each color is identified by a name as well as a number.

PANTONE® 19-1761 TCX	PANTONE® 19-1761 TCX	PANTONE® 19-1761 TCX	PANTONE® 19-1761 TCX
Tango Red	Tango Red	Tango Red	Tango Red

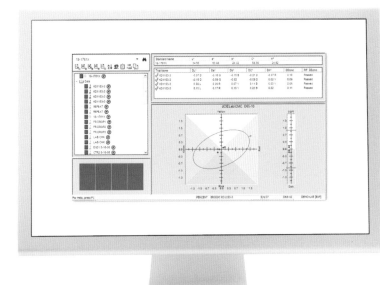

Pantone offers spectral data for all of its PANTONE® FASHION + HOME colors allowing today's textile labs to confirm color digitally.

The PANTONE® FASHION + HOME Color System offers a comprehensive range of colour standards with 1,925 cotton color chips chromatically arranged and numerically referenced.

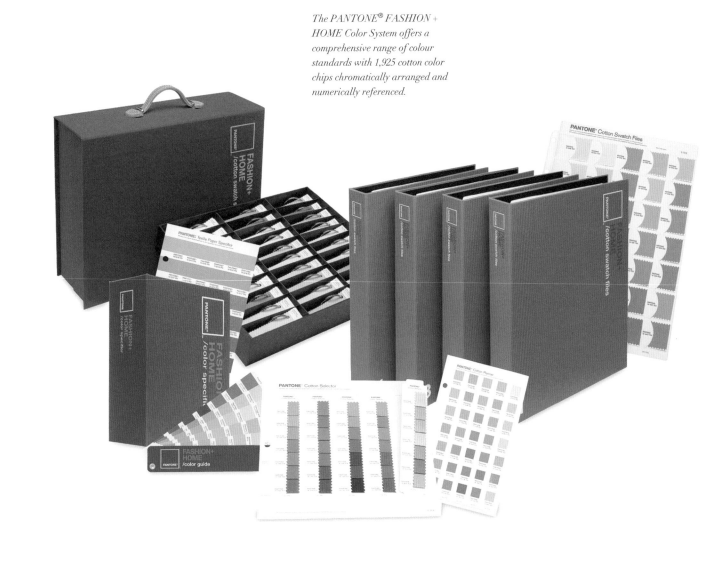

CHAPTER 4
UNDERSTANDING
COLOR CYCLES

FADS, TRENDS, AND CYCLES

Color forecasting is defined as the process of predicting the probable color and trend directions 18 to 24 months ahead of the selling season, but it is important to acknowledge that these trends exist within the context of color cycles; color trends and palettes do not exist in a vacuum. These cycles of colors, styles, or trends in fashion seem to have a sense of rhythm; they wax and wane, are forgotten about, and are eventually rediscovered and reinvented.

While **fads** are quick flashes of popularity that may bubble up from the street or through social networking or viral marketing, **trends** are less ephemeral, resulting from myriad cultural, social, political, and economic influences that interact to influence consumer preferences—and are expressed in a wide variety of fashion-related products over a season or two. Color cycles, however, are broader color movements that reflect long-term and more complex cultural forces.

"Color cycles refer to two phenomena: the periodic shifts in color preferences and the pattern of repetition in the popularity of colors," according to Evelyn Brannon, author of the 2005 book *Fashion Forecasting*. "Cycles last longer and are more predictable than trends, and trends are more enduring than fads," writes Jack Bredenfoerder, Design Director at Landor, in a 2009 blog entry.

Fads are hip, quirky, and sometimes extreme. Recent examples include legwarmers, harem pants, and Crocs plastic shoes. While fads often fizz like a carbonated drink and quickly go flat, occasionally one may evolve into a trend—it gets picked up by the media, enters the fashion vocabulary, and begins to gain respectability.

In men's underwear, for example, the use of color—and a tighter fit enhanced with the use of spandex (or elastane)—was considered a fad associated with the gay community. But beginning with Calvin Klein's billboards in the 1990s, and continuing with the launch of new brands such as Ginch Gonch and 2(X)ist on specialized Internet shopping sites, men gradually became more comfortable with fashion underwear.

Female shoppers also encouraged their male partners in the transformation of this fad into a trend, while at the same time the "metrosexual" mood of the decade inspired men to be more aware of fashion and their sexuality. Fashion trends such as low-slung jeans also made it fashionable for both men and women to show one's underwear. Today the use of bold color, pattern, and body-conscious design in men's underwear is more acceptable, particularly among younger consumers.

Another fad that became a trend and could now be called a cycle is the "Goth" look—skinny black jeans, black boots, aggressive silver jewelry, and dark makeup. While Goth subculture was originally an offshoot of the Punk, Indie, and New Romantics music scenes, its skinny black jeans and black boots have become classics for both men and women. Dark nail polish became mainstream with Chanel's Rouge Noir, launched in 1994 and worn by Uma Thurman in the Tarantino film *Pulp Fiction*, and was in vogue for the latter part of the Noughties. Interpretations of the Goth look continue to be seen at designer level and on the street.

The emergence of fast-fashion clothing chains such as Topshop, Forever 21, H&M, Primark, Zara, and Uniqlo have blurred the line between fads and trends with their ability to respond quickly to the consumer taste swings that seemingly come from the streets while at the same time offering versions of runway trends with commercial potential. Clothing that costs little and is disposed of after two or three wearings gives fashionistas quick access to legitimate designer trends as well as to fads that may be over very quickly.

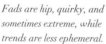

Fads are hip, quirky, and sometimes extreme, while trends are less ephemeral.

Originally a fad, the use of color, pattern, and body-conscious fit in men's underwear has become an accepted trend.

The "Goth" look emerged from the streets in the early 1980s, was legitimized by designers such as Vivienne Westwood and Karl Lagerfeld for Chanel, and has proven its longevity, becoming a fashion cycle.

THE LENGTH OF COLOR CYCLES

In contrast to fads and trends, cycles become defined over time, as recognizable color and fashion trends associated with the mood of the day become entrenched for a period. Think of the in-your-face brights (including fluorescents) and metallic embellishments of the 1980s that became emblematic of the era's economic boom and "power dressing." Introduced by diverse designers such as Christian Lacroix, Nolan Miller, and Stephen Sprouse, the penchant for bright color, bold pattern, and ostentatious accessories evolved, becoming the norm on US television dramas such as *Dynasty* and *Dallas* and eventually moving onto the street.

In any given period of time, there may be several color cycles co-existing. Some color cycles may last longer than others, reflecting the speed of cultural change in the larger world. In the mid-twentieth century color directions moved relatively slowly and a color could have a life span of about seven years before it saturated the market.

A major sociological, political, or economic event may trigger more rapid change than may normally occur. The stock market crash of 1987 finally brought an end to power dressing, and ushered in an era of "no-color" black, beige, and gray as an antidote to the excesses of the 1980s. While a minimalist palette was not the only color trend, technical fabrics, texture, and cut took precedence over color and pattern. Examples included Donna Karan's basic pieces in black and Calvin Klein's subtle neutrals, along with designers such as Helmut Lang and Jil Sander who limited their palettes primarily to black and white, and the monochromatic tones of the avant-garde Japanese designers such as Rei Kawakubo and Yohji Yamamoto. In 1989 Rifat Ozbek launched his influential all-white "new age" collection, bringing a decade of brash fashion to a quiet close.

The progression of cycles in color temperature—the warm or cool undertone of a hue or overall palette—can also be linked with global trends. The evolution of the PANTONE® FASHION + HOME Color System Color of the Year over the past few years saw a very warm Chili Pepper replaced in 2008 by a blue-cast purple (Blue Iris). In 2009 Mimosa yellow was a beacon of hope amidst a global recession, to be replaced by a more serene Turquoise in 2010.

Longer-term fashion cycles follow evolutionary style movement and can exist over periods as long as a century, according to Annette Lynch and Mitchell Strauss in *Changing Fashion*. Think of the inexorable movement into casual dressing, characterized by the popularization of the indigo-blue denim jean. Originally adopted from workwear by the young and anti-establishment, this cycle has co-existed with a number of fashion movements, from hippies to grunge to hip-hop and designer fashion; it spans the gamut of price points and age groups.

Many color specialists view color cycles as lasting around ten years; it is certainly convenient to define historical color cycles in terms of decades. While color cycles may be slower in a difficult economy, in general the pace of color cycles is increasing in speed, driven by fast fashion.

The indigo-blue denim jean cycle began in the 1950s and shows few signs of abating 60 years on.

PANTONE®
15-5519 TCX
Turquoise

PANTONE®
15-5519 TCX
Turquoise

PANTONE®
14-0848 TCX
Mimosa

PANTONE®
14-0848 TCX
Mimosa

PANTONE®
18-3943 TCX
Blue Iris

PANTONE®
18-3943 TCX
Blue Iris

PANTONE®
19-1557 TCX
Chili Pepper

PANTONE®
19-1557 TCX
Chili Pepper

The evolution of the PANTONE®
FASHION + HOME Color System
Color of the Year (Chili Pepper
2007, Blue Iris 2008, Mimosa
2009, and Turquoise 2010) presents
an interesting study of color
temperature cycles.

COLOR CYCLES BECOME SHORTER

With today's media infrastructure and social networking the pace has now quickened and a particular color or level of color may be commercially relevant for a few seasons at best. Inspired by the sustainability movement, green was touted as "the new black" by the media in 2006, and bright greens from apple to emerald were featured in fashion products. But while the sustainability movement carried forward, green as a wearable fashion shade had a relatively short life. Within a few seasons green had morphed into blue-greens and earthy brown-cast greens, and by 2008/2009 purples and reds dominated the palette.

The phenomenon of the shorter cycle is also linked to the cost of production, according to Wolfgang Pesendorfer of Northwestern University in his paper on "Design Innovation and Fashion Cycles." Fashion produced at a high fixed cost—such as couture—will sell at a high price, requiring that the design and color are fashionable over a long period. If production costs are low, as for today's fast-fashion retailers, then the window of popularity for a particular style and color will be short.

While cycles are getting shorter, we are also seeing more of the fad or maverick hue that features for a few weeks in a single season, inspired perhaps by a video or celebrity red-carpet appearance. Short-term colors often appear during the summer vacation season in items such as T-shirts, which are inexpensive and easy to produce, and many factories and production schedules have a gap in their time frames to accommodate these quick turnarounds.

Live streaming of Fashion Week presentations on the Internet, which began in earnest in 2010, may shorten the fashion cycle even more, circumventing fashion magazines and retailers by providing the consumer with the latest information. The design community has begun to question the timing of seasonal fashion shows, as well as the schedule for shipping clothing into the store months before the season actually commences. Some designers are in favor of keeping the show schedule for the trade, while adding a seasonal media presentation for the consumer.

The color forecaster should be familiar with past and current color cycles, their rhythms and timing, beginning with comparing the current palette with palettes from the past few seasons. The identification of cycles in color hue, value, chroma, and temperature and their underlying social, economic, and political drivers forms the backdrop against which the color forecaster will begin to develop the next new palette.

With lower production costs, today's fast fashion has a shorter life span than more expensive designer clothing.

Short-term "maverick" colors
may appear during the summer
vacation season in low-cost
items such as T-shirts.

WHAT DRIVES CYCLES IN COLOR PREFERENCES?

Unless clothing no longer fits or is worn out, most consumers do not purchase new clothes out of necessity, but because they want to be stylish or on-trend; the fashion business survives because consumers feel the need for something new. Color, of course, is an important point of differentiation that helps to designate an item as new or fashionable.

SIMMEL AND FASHION STATUS

Sociologists, economists, and historians have written a great deal about the forces (beyond need) that drive consumers to acquire fashion. One theory that is generally accepted is the **trickle-down theory**, first suggested in 1904 by the German sociologist Georg Simmel. Simmel theorized that fashion divided society into higher and lower classes, and that the lower classes imitated the higher classes by adopting their mode of dress. This in turn caused the upper classes to buy into new fashions in order to differentiate themselves from the underclass.

"Just as soon as the lower classes begin to copy their style, thereby crossing the line of demarcation the upper class has drawn and destroying the uniformity of their coherence, the upper classes turn away from this style and adopt a new one, which in its turn differentiates them from the masses," Simmel argued.

While today this elitist theory is considered somewhat simplistic, we still speak in terms of **aspirational fashion** as consumers seek to imitate the new royalty—celebrities—or try to elevate their own status by wearing something not yet seen at mass-market level. One tried-and-true marketing tactic is the practice of gifting celebrities with "swag" (free merchandise) in the hope of creating desire at the consumer level. A Mulberry handbag on the arm of Beyoncé or a pair of J-Brand jeans worn by Gwyneth Paltrow can generate success for the brand, aided by the celebrity-obsessed weekly fan/shopping magazines.

BLUMER AND COLLECTIVE SELECTION

A more egalitarian theory holds that consumers are more interested in things that are new and innovative than in imitating the style of a small and elite group. In 1969 the American sociologist Herbert Blumer proposed that fashion is the result of **collective selection**. Consumers make individual choices from competing styles through which collective fashion trends emerge that express the zeitgeist.

Simmel and others also saw the duality in consumer psychology that drives consumers to buy into fashion, becoming part of a trend, yet at the same time they seek to differentiate themselves, creating a new trend. "Two social tendencies are essential to the establishment of fashion, namely, the need of union on one hand and the need of isolation on the other," he wrote.

A recent article in the *Stanford Law Review* by Scott Hemphill and Jeannie Suk revisited this theory, referring to the participation in a group fashion movement as "flocking"*:* "…in fashion we observe the interaction of the tastes for differentiation and for flocking, or differentiation within flocking… it would not be fashion if only flocking behavior were present."

Sociologist Georg Simmel theorized that fashion was a symbol of status, and that the lower classes imitated the higher classes by adopting their mode of dress.

THE INFLUENCE OF STREET FASHION

The desire to stand out is responsible for fashion movements that "bubble up" from the streets. "Today, the group who sets the 'hip' is often likely to emerge from the streets, from youth cultures rather than from the elite at the top and mainstream of the social strata…in other words, fashion can and does 'bubble up' the social hierarchy from the bottom up to the status of high fashion," confirm John Dawson and Jung-Hee Lee in their 2004 book *International Retailing Plans and Strategies in Asia*.

One of the major fashion influences of the 1990s, hip-hop started on the urban streets in the 1970s as a music movement, became a trend, and appears to have settled in as a fashion cycle. Its baggy jeans, overstyled sneakers, track suits, hoodies, graphic T's, and bling were comingled with fashions from designers such as Versace, Hilfiger, and Polo Ralph Lauren.

Hip-hop colors—gritty, urban grays, rusts, and browns with splashes of athletic and graffiti brights—were incorporated into the color palettes of the 1990s. At its peak the look was translated by the likes of Juicy Couture and even Karl Lagerfeld, and the once-urban look was adopted by the fashion-conscious from Hollywood to the suburbs.

Contemporary trend guru, editor, and lecturer Martin Raymond is a major proponent of the **bubble-up theory**. He believes that individuals, not majorities, influence future trends, and that few consumers can actually articulate the reason for buying into a trend. "The new infect and impact on the old world, or the status quo, and by being there, by being close to others who share similar ideas and outlooks, hook up to them and are drawn towards them… so that alliances are formed, patterns created, opportunities and creative and cognitive leaps made," he writes in *The Tomorrow People*.

Hip-hop culture is a prime example of a fashion movement that "bubbled up" from the street.

THE FASHION PENDULUM

In contrast to Raymond's belief that fashion movements are spontaneous, other theorists see fashion cycles as slow **pendulum cycles**, swinging from one extreme the other, created by complex social forces. In 1958 economist Dwight Robinson speculated that an entire swing of the fashion pendulum spanned about a century, citing examples such as the exaggerated bustle and leg-of-mutton sleeves from Victorian times moving through the shirtwaist and hobble skirt of the Edwardian period and eventually into the pared-down silhouettes of the emancipated 1920s.

Robinson believed that the cause of fashion change was the psychological need for novelty. We can often discern the pendulum effect in color trends as they swing from cool to warm, shades to tints, pure hues to tones, and back again. (The PANTONE® FASHION + HOME Color System Color of the Year designation examined on p.89 is just one example.)

More recently, the statistical analysis of Lowe and Lowe found that past fashion cycles were relatively predictive of future fashion movements, but less so the further in the future one attempted to predict. However, they felt that "individual innovation and initiative," (e.g. on the part of influential fashion designers) also impact the long-term fashion cycle. In other words, while fashion moves in cycles, and we can look to past cycles to give an indication of future trends, there are always trendsetters who stand out and "rock the boat."

For example, in 2010 colors settled into a more conservative, classic and utilitarian cycle, influenced by the economic and political events of the previous two years. With the continuation of economic uncertainty, it seemed unlikely that the pendulum was ready to swing, and many designers chose to open their Spring 2011 shows with pristine white, a seemingly safe color. Miuccia Prada, however, introduced tropical, Latin-influenced brights for her collection. While the zeitgeist may not have indicated the advent of these colors, Prada's innovation could potentially function as a catalyst for change in the color cycle.

Economist Dwight Robinson speculated that fashion swings on a slow pendulum from one extreme to the other, as from the exaggerated mutton sleeves of the Victorian age to the short, spare flapper designs of the 1920s.

CONSUMERS AND TREND ADOPTION

All of these theories tell us that some consumers want to stand out, while others want to blend in. Like Martin Raymond in *The Tomorrow People,* Malcolm Gladwell utilizes this knowledge in *The Tipping Point.* Gladwell draws on the research of Everett Rogers that describes the rate of adoption of any innovation by various groups in a population. First published in 1962, Rogers' groundbreaking book *Diffusions of Innovations* pioneered the terms "tipping point" and "early adopters."

Rogers and Gladwell refer to those consumers with a strong drive for differentiation as "early adopters," those with more interest in being part of the tribe as "early majority," and consumers with little sense of innovation or differentiation as "late majority." "Innovators" are those creative types who move against the general fashion flow and help to drive newness (our boat-rockers), while "laggards" are the very last to adopt a new innovation.

Raymond's consumer definitions are similar. "Receptors" are those who pick up on innovations, while "reflectors" will try something new on personal recommendation. "Absorbers" take ideas and modify them to make them more acceptable to the "latents" or late majority. "Laggards" will eventually adopt an innovation because it is the path of least resistance, while "resistors" are entrenched and backward-looking.

Color and design cycles do not rise and fall because designers and color forecasters decide the time is right, but because consumers tire of the status quo and seek out the new. While we expect to see new color and fashion ideas on the designer runways, the truth is that many of their ideas come from the streets, or are simply recycled. Ruth La Ferla writes in the *New York Times*, "Today, in place of a linear progression in either direction, there is a continuous cycle of eddying currents."

While fashion and color cycles are driven by socioeconomic trends, they also reflect consumers' desire to imitate a celebrity or aspirational lifestyle, and the need to be part of a fashion tribe as well as to differentiate. Understanding human behavior in this light will assist the color forecaster in developing a seasonal palette within the context of color cycles.

The desire to be part of the trend and the desire to differentiate oneself exist in various proportions across the spectrum of consumers.

Consumers who buy into fashion trends as part of a tribe, wearing similarly stylish clothing or sporting signature haircuts, are known as "the early majority" or "reflectors."

THE BELL CURVE OF COLOR CYCLES

Color forecasters can introduce colors and new ways of using them, but a color does not become popular overnight. The forecaster must look at each season in terms of emerging, current, and post-peak trends within a color cycle, in order to ascertain when best to introduce a new color. "So much of what is going to happen in the future is intimately connected to and influenced by the present and the past," explains Roseann Forde of Fordecasting.

Colors and color palettes have a life cycle; from the introduction of a hue to the point where the color has been used extensively and across different product areas. The life cycle of a color, like that of a fashion cycle, can be visualized as a **bell curve**. In 1928 Paul Nystrom, a professor of marketing at Columbia University, demonstrated the life cycle of a fashion trend on a simple graph, with time plotted on the horizontal axis and consumer acceptance of a product on the vertical axis.

At the beginning of the curve, new color directions and applications are introduced and test-marketed, hopefully to be accepted by the early adopters. Product developers and retail buyers then adopt the color for their products, and the color is picked up by the early majority—as we visualize the graph of the bell curve starting to climb. As the color reaches the mass market where it is adopted by the so-called late majority, the bell curve peaks and begins to fall. Now the color is moved to the markdown racks and discounters and is considered post-peak. Gradually the color or color family will disappear, to be replaced by a new color cycle.

While fashion and color cycles are typically bell-shaped, there can be some variation depending on the rate of a movement's acceptance and decline. For example, the curve for a fad may rise quickly and fall off sharply, while the curve for a classic fashion or "basic" may flatten out into a broad and lengthy shape. Basics are products such as T-shirts, cardigans, or Oxford button-down shirts that are sold for years with few style changes (although the clever use of color can certainly give them seasonal fashion appeal.)

Raymond also writes about a break called the **trend chasm** (a phrase first coined by Geoffrey Moore in *Crossing the Chasm*) on the upward swing of the bell curve. This theoretical black hole is the point "where most trends die because they are far too new for the mainstream to bother with."

New color directions can take years to become established. There is usually a time lag from when a color has been introduced as part of a cutting-edge collection, to the recognition of the color as commercially acceptable and mainstream. One example would be Christian Louboutin's high-end shoes with red soles. Louboutin's nail-lacquer red sole was introduced in 1992, setting his luxury shoes apart from the competition. By the Noughties his stilettos became the favorite of Hollywood and real-life royalty, and by 2007 high-street imitations drove him to file for a patent for the shiny red soles. In 2011 the red sole remains a status symbol for shoe-lovers, with faux Louboutins and "red-sole kits" for sale on the Internet.

The life cycle of a color or color family is extended when it crosses over to other product areas. A color trend may begin in fashion apparel, and travel to accessories, beauty, interiors, automotive, and technology, where the cycle of color development may be longer—the lead time for automotive colors is three to four years. The fashion business in turn will also take note of macrotrends in these fields.

An interesting example of a general color trend infiltrating fashion apparel is the recent rise of yellow as a commercially acceptable color in contemporary fashion. At a saturated level, it is a color that is frequently used in active sportswear, as in the leader's jersey for cycling's Tour de France; or in safety wear because of its visibility. Yellow has always had a more significant presence in interiors, but in fashion apparel it has usually shown up in less intense versions, used primarily as an accent color.

Recently, shades of sharp, fresh yellow have become more important in designer fashion (at Burberry Prorsum in 2005 and Dries Van Noten in 2006, for example) and on the red carpet (Kate Moss in 2004 and Reese Witherspoon in 2007) as well as in the home and interiors markets.

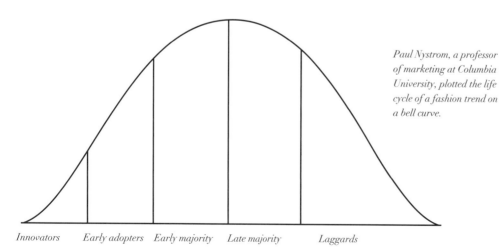

Paul Nystrom, a professor of marketing at Columbia University, plotted the life cycle of a fashion trend on a bell curve.

Innovators   Early adopters   Early majority   Late majority   Laggards

Yellow, which is traditionally used in safety and sport applications, has recently enjoyed a cycle of popularity in contemporary fashion.

Christian Louboutin's signature red soles were introduced in 1992; over a 15-year time span they were adopted by celebrities, spawning high-street imitations, and were patented by the designer in 2007.

Inspired by designers such as Burberry Prorsum in 2005 and Dries Van Noten in 2006, yellow has become a favorite with celebrities on the red carpet. PANTONE 14-0848 Mimosa yellow was selected as the 2009 PANTONE Color of the Year.

TRADITION IN COLOR CYCLES

In addition to cycles of color hue, value, chroma, or temperature, there are traditional seasonal color cycles and classic palettes that the color forecaster should take into consideration. Color palettes tend to be light and bright in spring and summer, and rich and dark in fall and winter, although there are always some exceptions.

There are also certain events within the calendar year that influence palettes for seasonal collections. In the West, these include red, pink, and black for Valentine's Day intimate apparel; back-to-school palettes in fall that are usually inspired by school colors; and winter (Christmas) holiday colors of reds, winter whites, and black, including lots of sparkle and metallics.

Some colors are considered classics and are always in style: black, gray, navy, red, khaki tan, white, and cream are always considered chic and tasteful. Interestingly these colors are often utilized by couturiers and designers in addition to more offbeat, forward colors to round out their collections. This may be in part because of the price of fashion at this level, or because these colors will emphasize the texture and finish of a complex fabric or the cut of a radical design.

Think of Chanel's knitwear and "little black dress," or the nondescript minimalist neutrals of a Calvin Klein collection, or the dramatic all-black silhouettes of Yamamoto, Miyake, and Kawakubo, or of Gaultier's nautical stripes. The couturier Madeleine Vionnet relied on pure, solid colors such as black, white, and red to emphasize the clever seaming of her bias-cut creations, as well as on beige and flesh tones to capture the drape of fabric on the body. Valentino and Halston were both known for their signature reds, and Donna Karan consistently emphasizes black in her designer collections.

Other designers are known for colors that may not be considered classic but are nevertheless signature and inspirational. In 1936 Elsa Schiaparelli launched shocking pink, a color somewhere between fuchsia and red. It became the hallmark of her couture house, and has become so thoroughly accepted that it is no longer "shocking." Couturier Jeanne Lanvin's signature color was cornflower blue, while pink and gray are the signature colors of the house of Dior.

Certain color cycles are also linked to cyclical events such as the Olympic Games and other major sports events, where the winning team's colors may enjoy a season of popularity. The 2010 FIFA World Cup in South Africa inspired the popularity of an African color palette of red, yellow, green, and black for sports clothing. Election campaigns and the colors of national flags also drive cycles in color.

In times of international conflict, the colors of military uniforms such as navy, gray, khaki tan, and olive drab, along with camouflage patterns using these colors, are often utilized in civilian fashion. Fashion runways and magazines in early 2010 featured these colors in a wide range of military-inspired field coats, flight jackets, and trench-coat styling.

Color popularity can be linked to team colors for cyclical events such as the FIFA World Cup and the Olympic Games.

Military colors are often used in civilian fashion, especially in times of conflict; here from Dries Van Noten's Fall/Winter 2010 collection.

Designers are often known for colors that may not be considered classic, but become the signature of the house, such as Elsa Schiaparelli's shocking pink.

HISTORICAL COLOR CYCLES

With the exception of the few true innovators, many of the "new" styles and colors we see at retail each season take inspiration from historical fashion cycles. Designers and fashion forecasters mine museums and vintage stores for inspiration, and old fashion magazines and journals are particularly prized. Significant fashion cycles are generally attached to an iconic palette, which color forecasters can revisit and rework when developing new palettes. Understanding the cyclical nature of color and fashion within its socioeconomic context can also help us to predict when a particular use of color will come back into vogue—when the pendulum will swing back.

As discussed in Chapter 2 (see p.40) the use of color to drive fashion trends gained momentum with the discovery of aniline dyes by William Henry Perkin in 1856. These synthetic colors were shockingly new and exciting to the demure Victorians. Following the death of Prince Albert in 1861, however, many lower and middle class women emulated Queen Victoria's black mourning clothes.

Then from around the 1860s, William Morris instigated the Aesthetic, or Arts and Crafts, movement which admired Medieval and Renaissance design in reaction to cheaply manufactured machine-made products, Victorian frippery, and synthetic dyestuffs. Morris and his colleagues reinstated natural dyestuffs and worked in hand woodblock printing rather than commercial roller printing. Morris' colors, prints, tapestries, and embroidery patterns periodically re-emerge as design influences for fashion and interiors.

In the early twentieth century, French designer Paul Poiret revolutionized the fashion palette with his use of bright, opulent, theatrical shades and patterns. Inspired by Orientalism and the **Ballet Russes**, his sense of color celebrated the seraglios of the East and the painters of the Fauvist movement. He rebelled against the soft colors of the age, writing, "I threw into this sheepcote a few rough wolves: reds, greens, violets, royal blues that made all the rest sing aloud."

Poiret not only exerted an enormous influence on the fashion of the day, but he raised the bar in terms of the designer as a celebrity and as an iconic brand. Howard Koda of New York's Metropolitan Museum of Art commented, "Poiret… envisioned a 'total lifestyle' that extended from how [a woman] dressed and what fragrance she wore to how she decorated her home—an approach reflected in the strategies of many of today's fashion houses."

At the opposite end of the spectrum but equally influential a decade later was the fashion of Coco Chanel, whose uncluttered lines, sporty jersey fabric, and simple palette of black, navy, white, and variations on beige appealed to women's practicality during the years of World War I. Chanel's approach to color lives on today.

Led by William Morris in the 1870s and 1880s, the Arts and Crafts movement included the prints of Thomas Wardle and reinstated natural dyestuffs and woodblock printing.

Coco Chanel's simple palette lives on in the little black dresses and "classic" colors chosen by elegant women year after year.

In the early 1900s French designer Paul Poiret challenged establishment fashion design with his opulent, Eastern-inspired colors and patterns.

LE POUF

ROBE DU SOIR, DE PAUL POIRET

N° 7 de la Gazette. Année 1924 Planche 38
Modèle déposé. Reproduction interdite.

-A.E MARTY-

THE TWENTIETH CENTURY AND BEYOND

Each decade since has had its iconic trends, but the 1960s were especially memorable, with the kind of societal changes that flew in the face of establishment fashion cycles. This was the period when individual innovation and initiative began to make a real difference, and new trends didn't just bubble—they percolated up from the streets.

This prosperous and creative era was characterized by bright "Pop Art" colors and fluorescents, young designers, and swinging London-inspired fashion. Technical developments in synthetic textiles and dyestuffs also increased the depth and range of achievable colors.

As we have seen, less ostentatious lifestyles returned in the late 1980s along with a growing consciousness of ecological concerns, such as the harmful by-products of textile dyeing. This early environmental movement drove the development of undyed, naturally colored fibers such as Foxfibre® cotton that grew in tones of green and brown, as well as unbleached wools and silks in natural tones of gray and beige.

While the prosperity of the Noughties once again brought us strong and experimental color, an event like that of the economic crisis of late 2008 generally portends the beginning of a new color cycle. Indeed color forecasts for 2011 are focused on wearable classics such as black, gray, navy, red, ivory, and khaki, as well as familiar, saleable favorites that are comforting—mid-blues, soft pinks, warm browns, camels, and earth tones.

Since the end of the Noughties there is also a continuing movement back into natural and organic fibers and dyestuffs, reycycled textiles, and the handcrafted techniques of William Morris. The runways for Fall 2010 included quilting, tapestries, embroideries, and collages of different fabrics.

The 1960s was an era of bright fluorescent colors and Pop Art patterns epitomized by London-inspired fashion.

The vast leap forward in materials technology since the 1960s space race has seen the emergence of reflective, luminous, fluorescent, and morphing pigments.

James Laver, an author and art historian (Keeper in the Department of Engraving, Illustration and Design at the Victoria & Albert Museum from 1938 to 1959) was well known for his contributions to the field of fashion history. In 1937 he outlined Laver's Law, a timeline of fashion's cycles that explains how historical fashion trends and colors seem to reappear periodically. In retrospect his descriptions are somewhat amusing.

Indecent	10 years before its time
Shameless	5 years before its time
Outré (Daring)	1 year before its time
Smart	Current Fashion
Dowdy	1 year after its time
Hideous	10 years after its time
Ridiculous	20 years after its time
Amusing	30 years after its time
Quaint	50 years after its time
Charming	70 years after its time
Romantic	100 years after its time
Beautiful	150 years after its time

As we can see, fashion colors and trends are constantly recycled. The Aesthetics celebrated Medieval and Renaissance dress, the Art Deco movement referenced Ancient Egyptian design, while the Ballet Russes were an inspiration for Paul Poiret in the early 1900s as well as for the 2009 collections of Marc Jacobs, Karl Lagerfeld, and Monique Lhuillier. In Fall 2009 we saw fluorescent brights, big shoulders, and leggings from the 1980s, and recently magazines have begun to tout a return to the fashions of the 1990s.

Color forecasters will benefit from an understanding of historical color cycles, not only in making the associations between historical events and trends in apparel, but in having a visual repertoire to draw upon when developing contemporary color palettes.

Since the end of the Noughties there has been a movement back into natural and organic fibers and dyestuffs, as well as a renewed interest in handcrafted techniques.

HISTORICAL COLOR CYCLES IN WESTERN FASHION FROM 1850

Starting with the development of synthetic dyes in 1856, color began to drive trends in fashion and became associated with particular personalities, designers, and social or artistic movements that we still reference today.

Queen Victoria dies 1901; light and refreshing pastels usher in Belle Epoque

Ballet Russes, Orientalism, Art Nouveau, and Expressionism inspire Paul Poiret's radical vibrant palette during century's first decade

War years see simpler palette inspired by Chanel: black, navy, white, and beige

Depression colors: navy, beige, dusty mauve, and gray contrast with fantasy world of couture and movie-star glamour

Surrealism, Schiaparelli's shocking pink, Hartnell's white wardrobe for the Queen

World War II colors are utilitarian and patriotic: nautical red, white, and blue along with uniform greens and khakis

Era of youth, prosperity, and creativity. Young designers and swinging London drive bright, kaleidoscopic pop colors and fashions

In Paris the young designers rebel against the couture and begin designing ready-to-wear

Hippies and the drug culture bring us flower power, psychedelia, and unusual color mixes

Modern art and space-age materials inspire primary colors, bold graphics, and glossy, metallic colors

| 1850–1900 | 1900–1920 | 1920–1930 | 1930–1945 | 1945–1960 | 1960–1970 |

Aniline dyes discovered by William Henry Perkin, 1856. Mauveine purple leads to brilliant colors such as apple green, royal blue, mandarin

Prince Albert dies 1861. Queen Victoria wears mourning for remainder of her life; black, gray, and dull purple become colors of the middle classes

1860s onward, William Morris establishes Aesthetic, or Arts and Crafts, movement; return to natural dyestuffs such as indigo and madder

Post war boom, women more liberated. Art Deco, Egyptian design, and Cubism inspire brighter, cleaner, modern colors: cream, Nile green, gold, coral, and turquoise

World plunged into economic depression, 1929

Post war period brings Dior's New Look, reviving interest in fashion

While Europe rebuilds, US experiences economic boom. 1950s colors are cheerful and optimistic with a technical edge: turquoise, chartreuse, and flamingo pink

Technical developments in fibers and dyestuffs encourage brighter, more experimental colors

Materialism of 1980s is reflected in black with flashes of bright and opulent color. Metallics and gaudy jewelry inspire the term "material girl"

Madonna and *Flashdance* inspire mix of punk, vintage, and exercise gear including fluorescent spandex leggings, black leather and lace, oversized tops

Hip-hop emerges as urban music and fashion movement. Bright colors inspired by athletic teams and African culture mix with heavy gold jewelry and designer sneakers

Skater fashion urbanizes surf lifestyle, adding graffiti prints and computerized art

Consumers turn toward more spiritual and environmental pursuits; soft blues, silvery neutrals, white

Darwin's bicentenary inspires renewed appreciation of natural world; green touted as the new black

Interest in Eastern cultures brings more exotic use of color. Rich purples, reds, yellows, hot pinks, metalllics, and embellishments rule as economy expands mid-decade. Celebrities and colorful designer handbags epitomize the era

War in Middle East sees continued interest in military colors and camouflage. Recession hits in 2008, inspiring return to utilitarian basics, neutrals, and the tasteful tried-and-true

Icons of 1950s femininity inspire pretty pastels and optimistic brights

1970–1980   1980–1990   1990–2000   2000–2010

Era of disco and synthetic clothing; colors clash and include funky browns, oranges, avocados, purples, and acid shades

YSL's Russian collection drives explosion of prints and patterns and renewed interest in Eastern cultures, with a resurgence of red and jewel tones

Punk and a harsher perspective influence end of 1970s. Punk broadens its appeal in 1980s, adding plaids and bright synthetic colors to its signature black leather

Minimalism returns as 1987 stock market crash brings an end to bling. Designers feature black and neutrals

Gray and beige are strong as growing sense of the environment sees renewed interest in natural fibers. Color used monochromatically in head-to-toe ensembles

Anti-fashion movement extends to grunge, with thrift store looks and flannel; colors are neutral, earthy, and muted

CHAPTER 5
COLOR FORECASTING
TOOLS AND
METHODOLOGIES

The development of a seasonal palette is an ongoing process, grounded in the palette of the previous season.

BEGINNING THE COLOR FORECASTING PROCESS

By now it is clear that the process of color forecasting is a complex one, involving a knowledge base in color theory and cycles; vigilant observation of social, cultural, political, and economic trends; and the intangible contributions of inspiration and intuition. It is not enough for the student of color forecasting to "love fashion" or "enjoy playing with color." Building a seasonal color palette requires the right tools, an open mind, a disciplined approach to research, and the practice of one's craft.

Most people who work in color forecasting are trained in art and design and usually possess a natural creativity that is utilized in their jobs. However, color forecasting is a business and, as we have seen, a critical component of the fashion and design industry. The color practitioner has to strike a balance between being inspirational in order to attract the consumer, being objective in observing the general climate, and being methodical in assessing how color concepts can be applied.

There are no hard and fast rules governing methodologies, and each forecaster will approach the season in a slightly different manner. As trend and product development consultant Fran

Yoshioka puts it, "It's a highly individualized business with creativity and innovation being so personal and emotional—no two people will view, analyze, interpret, and create a color palette in the same way."

Most professional color forecasters view the development of a seasonal palette as an ongoing process, grounded in the palette of the previous season, but moving forward to fit the cultural zeitgeist of current and upcoming times. The idea of jumping into this swiftly flowing and often turbulent stream can be intimidating to the student or new graduate who wishes to practice trend development, which by its very nature is fluid rather than static. Where does the process begin?

Tim Brown, CEO of IDEO design and innovation consultancy and author of *Change by Design: How Design Thinking Transforms Organizations and Inspires Innovations*, tells us, "The myth of innovation is that brilliant ideas leap fully formed from the minds of geniuses. The reality is that most innovations come from a process of rigorous examination through which great ideas are identified and developed before being realized as new offerings and capabilities." In similar fashion, an inspiring and spot-on color palette does not spring fully developed from the mind of the color forecaster, even one who is thoroughly practiced and immersed in the world of fashion.

Beautiful images from nature, research in local markets, or trips overseas can inspire new ways with color.

A color palette does not spring fully developed from the mind of the color forecaster, but begins with one or more inspirations.

A creative store window such as Selfridge's *Alice in Wonderland* display may trigger an idea.

Armed with an understanding of the target customer and the success or failure of the previous season's trends, the color forecaster begins the season with one or more inspirations. Pat Tunsky of The Doneger Group describes taking the first step this way: "I sometimes start with an image of a garden, a room that is decorated in an interesting way, or a painting or a photograph that inspires me to think of a color story that I have not done recently. Sometimes I am inspired by a creative store window background. My European research trips always prove to be an inspirational 'jump start.'"

It is also important that these inspirations, no matter how beautiful, relate somehow to the spirit of the times. "Very different things can feel new and right—an exhibition or whatever, but it does need to fit the zeitgeist," insists UK design consultant Joanna Bowring. However, it is difficult to say whether the forecaster must consciously make an effort to choose inspiration that fits the current zeitgeist, or whether the experienced forecaster gravitates to timely inspiration through intuition based on practice.

In addition to inspiration, Lindsey Riley of UK color consultancy Insight maintains, "very important also is to research and analyze what is actually happening at the shows and retail, and client feedback in order to project forward. I see it as an iceberg. The creativity and inspiration are the tip that shows, supported on fact, experience, and tons of research that makes up the bulk below."

East Central Studio's principal Sandy McLennan believes inspiration and zeitgeist are intrinsically linked. "It is always worth balancing 'future gazing' with current realities—although we are always talking about two years out so you have to imagine a different landscape and build on ideas that make you 'look', that attract you naturally. Over the years you tune your taste and feel for newness and totally rely on that for the key parts of a new color proposal."

Building a beautiful palette requires creativity backed up with research, analysis, and experience.

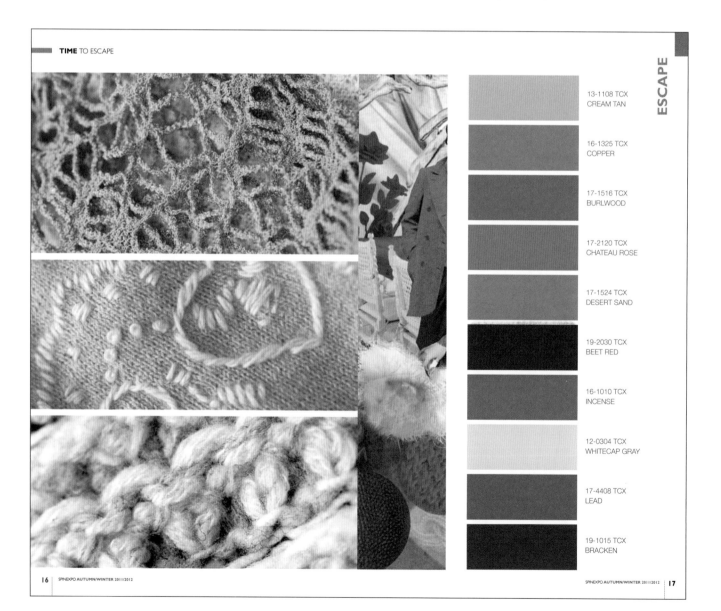

Inspiration

THE TREND:
FAIRYTALES, FABLES AND
NURSERY
RHYMES

Tim Walker

Nursery Rhymes

- Little Red Riding Hood
- Little Miss Muffet
- Little Bow Peep
- Jack And Jill
- Repunzel
- Goldie Locks
- Humpty Dumpty
- Hansel and Gretal

Jean Charles De Castelbajac

David La Chapelle

Galliano

Bernhard Willhelem

It is important that inspiration fits the current zeitgeist, as shown by this brainstorm board from a student workshop at UCA Rochester.

THE PRACTICE OF OBSERVATION

Seeking inspiration and tracking the cultural zeitgeist through ongoing and incessant observation is a basic requirement for the color forecaster. In addition to observing the visual culture that feeds new ideas into fashion, it is also important to be able to put the information into consumer-driven context. While the political, social, and economic events in our ever-more-connected world may seem unrelated to fashion, they have a definite domino effect on the lifestyles, mindsets, and purchasing choices of consumers.

Transitioning from the original inspiration to the next step— observation—can be a very personalized process. The ongoing process of inspiration and intuition generates mixed information that usually requires a catalyst to pull everything together in a coherent manner. This may be as immediate as a newsflash, cultural event, or a particular visual that encapsulates all of the

elements. At this point the designer or forecaster must take the personal or subjective inspiration and interpret it objectively in the context of the intended product or market by using observation of the culture and current events.

For example, in 2006, Tate Britain held an exhibition called "Gothic Nightmares" featuring fantastic, erotic, and horror-filled paintings from the dark imaginations of late eighteenth- and nineteenth-century Romantics such as Wiliam Blake and Henry Fuseli. While the trend forecaster might have found the show itself artistically inspiring, it became more meaningful upon observation of the current culture's fascination with fantasy, such as the Harry Potter and *Twilight* books and movies, and the resurgence of Goth culture among the young.

Another example was the celebration of Darwin's bicentenary in 2009 (see also Chapter 1, p.21). Exhibitions and programs celebrating this became much more relevant when viewed in the context of present-day climate change.

RECORD YOUR OBSERVATIONS

A notebook or diary where one can record observations should not be confined to the written word. Photographs are invaluable, as are sketches and tactile collectible items such as objects from nature, yarns, ribbons, paper wrappings, postcards, seed packets, cosmetics, color chips, fabric swatches, video grabs, and anything else that catches the eye or plucks at the heartstrings.

Sir Paul Smith, known for his collection of inspirational objects, calls this his "magpie mentality." "Every thought could come in handy. It might turn out to be rubbish, but you won't know unless you write it down," he advises.

Cutting and pasting should be as much a part of the notebook as the written word. "Whenever I see something, I make a note of it, take a picture, or create some other visual, attach a color to it and create an ongoing file to review when I need to formalize a project," explains Carole D'Arconte of Carole D'Arconte LLC, formerly director of forecasting company Color Portfolio.

According to McLennan, "It's always a personal approach. I start with some words that are working around in my head—expand them into a very abstract narrative and allow a visual identity to form—then it is a very hands-on process—making up little pieces of work, taking photographs, painting, and dyeing—or just finding and matching."

As a color forecaster matures, collected files of larger bits of information will need to be archived, such as old color cards, magazine pages, indigenous art and textiles, book and album covers, etc. Not only will this visual information contribute to an understanding of the zeitgeist, but over time the collection will serve as archival references of cycles in color and design, to be used for building new storyboards and palettes.

Over time a "magpie mentality" will yield a rich archive of inspiration and information to be used in building future storyboards and palettes.

This student project illustrates the inspiration that comes from tactile collectible items such as yarns, ribbons, buttons, and wrappings.

Keeping a notebook is a must for the fashion forecaster, and can include photos and collectible items as well as written observations and impressions.

A notebook will assist in making the link between personal inspirations and current events in the wider world.

STUDY DESIGNER COLLECTIONS

Studying magazine and video reports of the designer collections are an important component of the color forecaster's methodology. The designer ready-to-wear collections, held for Spring and Fall six months in advance of each retail season, are closely watched by fast-fashion retailers, who will often interpret designer color and trend direction in time for the season.

For the color forecaster working 18–24 months in advance, the international runways can help confirm the current seasonal palette for clients or particular applications. For example, Viktor & Rolf's Fall 2010 "Paint it Black" menswear collection confirmed the season's move into blackened color presaged by the popular fascination with fantasy and horror, and by the economic crises two years earlier. The use of black, gray, petrol blues, and dark browns prevailed in many of the other menswear collections as well, such as Bottega Veneta, YSL, Dior, and Gucci.

More importantly, the often outlandish themes or signature colors of some of these international designer collections can inspire ideas for the development of a theme, story, or philosophy for a future palette, or launch a particular color family into the commercial marketplace. The late designer Alexander McQueen's themes, from the Highlands to Transylvania, from snow globes to the dark side of Victorian life, were glorious fodder for color and trend development.

The odd color combinations of Miuccia Prada, Dries Van Noten, and Consuelo Castiglioni at Marni at the beginning of the Noughties changed the way we use color today. And the rule-breaking use of color by masters such as Poiret and Saint Laurent is frequently referenced by designers and color forecasters in creating new palettes.

Botega Veneta's Fall/Winter 2010 collection, held six months in advance of the season, confirmed color forecasters' predictions for somber menswear colors; the seasonal runways regularly inspire fast-fashion interpretations.

An unusual color combination from Dries Van Noten's Fall/Winter 2000 collection continues to inspire the way we use color today.

The outlandishly themed collections created by designers such as Alexander McQueen (here, Fall/Winter 2006) can inspire ideas for future palettes, or launch a particular color family into the commercial marketplace.

NETWORKING AND THE WIDER WORLD

The practice of observation should extend to the wider world. Look at and listen to what is happening in music, sports, advertising, foods, brand perception, social networking, business management, finance, politics, industry, and all the events and products that touch the lives of consumers.

Being part of a network of creative people enables these efforts. Artists, writers, musicians, philosophers, product developers, marketers, and all types of designers will contribute to the color forecaster's growing ideas file of inspiration and observation.

While a traditional network is centralized, Martin Raymond utilizes the concept of a **distributive network**—one that is flattened and conversational, a cluster of creative types. In *The Tomorrow People* he describes this as a network that "allows ideas, innovation, change and newness to flow through it in a way that encourages creativity and promotes an atmosphere where the best kind of cognitive leaps can, and usually do, take place." While social networking and blogs provide cultural insights from the wider world at any hour of the day, sharing observations and inspirations within a trusted and collaborative network cannot be replaced.

In order to observe properly, the forecaster needs to walk the streets, visit the neighborhoods, shop the markets, chat in the cafés, attend the events. Don't just look—interact. Martin Raymond calls this **brailing**—reading, scanning, or engaging with the world around us in a tactile and hands-on way. "Listen, look, record, absorb, remember, report and learn, then extrapolate," he advises.

Attending shows and openings such as the Free Range Art & Design Show during London's Graduate Fashion Week allows the forecaster to engage with the world in a tactile and hands-on way.

JOIN PROFESSIONAL ORGANIZATIONS

Participation in some of the organized color councils such as the British Textile Colour Group (BTCG), Intercolor, or Color Marketing Group, is an excellent way to network as well as to confirm observations. These committees of color professionals develop palettes through a process of presenting, comparing, and analyzing the inspirations, observations, and data gathered by the members of the group. This exchange of information with colleagues can be invaluable.

In some organizations, such as Color Marketing Group, members are asked to bring their notebooks, texts, references from nature or manufactured items, tear sheets, or photographs, etc. The group then works together to build storyboards and a palette.

The BTCG and Intercolor tend to present in storyboard or mood board format, some more finished than others. These are a combination of primary research photos, tear sheets, fabric, yarn, and paper samples. After discussion and consensus, a curatorial team develops a palette of several groups, along with visuals, text, and Pantone® color matches.

Pascaline Wilhelm, Fashion Director of Première Vision, describes the process of the fair's color and trend concertation (committee). "All arrive with color palettes and explain each concept… we are trying to work and explain the importance of color for the season. We use a great deal of words but few colors. A too-large color palette confuses clients; the work is about the main directions, not specific shades."

During the seasonal meetings of the British Textile Colour Group, storyboards are presented, points of consilience are discussed, and the color stories to be developed for the future season are identified.

Participation in organized color councils (here Color Marketing Group) made up of professional color managers from a wide range of products helps to confirm observations and clarify the influence of trends on color direction.

MARKET DATA AND ANALYSIS

In observing the culture, the trend forecaster may wish to consider marketing data such as demographics and lifestyle trends for the target customer. This data can include age group, education, income, population distribution, and cultural identification, using quantitative and qualitative measurements garnered through market research, consumer group surveys, and street questionnaires. These are important tools in identifying the consumer aspirations and spending patterns for market projections. Such information is accessible through subscription (and sometimes on the Internet) from organizations such as Retail Forward, NPD Fashionworld, Mintel, WGSN, Just-Style, View Network, and others.

In some societies the opportunity to measure populations through a national census poll exists on a cyclical basis. In the US, national retailers such as Walmart, Target, and Chico's paid close attention to the 2010 census, which would have influenced their marketing campaigns, location of new stores, or store closures, and assisted them in tailoring merchandise offerings to suit local tastes.

Large retailers and brands will monitor sales trends very closely and adjust new developments accordingly. However, because color is only one of many variable components in fashion, and taste is very subjective, it is often difficult to pinpoint why a garment sells—or does not.

The forecaster must take care not to rely too heavily on hard data, which will necessarily measure a trend at its peak, at the expense of inspiration, observation, and intuition. Census data can only tell us what and where we are now, not where we will be in two years. While large, mid-, and mass-market brands and retailers may feel more secure with hard data that defines the peak of the bell curve (see p.96) in order to maximize sales, this information is unlikely to be forward enough for the true forecaster.

"Companies need to be courageous in experimenting with brand perceptions and rely less heavily on testing and research, which tend to nullify originality," according to Jason Little, a creative director at Landor.

Martin Raymond believes that "focus groups that are used to determine trends seldom offer up anything except answers we already know… because what we are attempting to uncover or 'measure' is part of the irrational world." Remember, the color forecaster may be working as far as two years ahead of the retail season, and needs to project future trends as well as understand the current ones.

DESIGN THINKING: FROM OBSERVATION TO CONCEPT

The wealth of information and experiences gathered and recorded may at first seem unrelated and confusing. This is perhaps the most difficult part of the process, the point at which the color forecaster must use a combination of design thinking and analytical skills to make sense of it all, then apply these learnings to the development of a color palette. As Robyn Waters writes in *The Trendmaster's Guide*, "You have to use your instinct, intuition and your heart to figure out what those observations are pointing to."

In a general sense, **design thinking** is defined by Tim Brown as a collaborative process by which the designer's sensibilities and methods are employed to match people's needs with what is technically feasible and a viable business strategy. What does this mean to color forecasting? Design thinking is the process by which the inspiration and gathered data are analyzed, sorted, and synthesized into a clear color message that can be applied to the intended products (technically feasible) and will fit the brand identity, appeal to the consumer, and drive sales (a viable business strategy).

Brown goes on to point out that design thinking is different and can feel uncomfortable, because it is not necessarily rational or orderly. Design thinking includes "divergence," which means we are creating choices, followed by "convergence," where we are making choices. Divergence is frustrating, he explains, because "it almost feels like you are going backwards and getting further away from the answer but this is the essence of creativity."

A storyboard from a first-year student group workshop illustrates the process of observing, collecting, and recording a wide range of visual influences.

STORYBOARDS

Because design thinking tells a story in a visual way, the favorite tool of designers and color forecasters is the storyboard. Large pieces of blank white cardboard, foam board, or canvas will work and are transportable. If one is lucky enough to have a workspace with a large blank wall, covering and using the wall as a giant palette or pin-up board is an alternative way to arrange, display and study one's accumulation of inspirations and observations. This will allow the flexibility to move a collection into different groupings as the relevance of inspirations and observations waxes and wanes with new ideas, before concepts are finalized on the storyboards.

Make groupings of your collection in an ongoing fashion; notice what works together, what creates tension, and what stands alone. For example, if you were working in the Spring of 2010 to gather information for the palette of Spring 2012, you might have pinned up headlines about the UK austerity budget and the Eurozone financial crisis, the BP oil-rig disaster, and the new conservatism exemplified by the Tea Party movement in the US. References to cooking and the whole foods movement might have inspired you, along with shots of organic or sustainable fashion. You might have added photos or the exhibition notes from the V&A's Quilts or Grace Kelly shows, along with an ethnic scarf from a street market or a pin up of Lady Gaga.

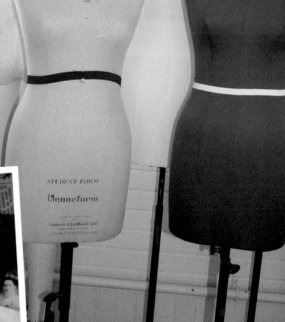

The color forecaster must use analytical skills and design thinking to make sense of seemingly unrelated images and information.

All of our inspirations, observations, and information must be broken down, taken apart, and put back together again in an ongoing process that may change several times before the new color direction, theme, or story emerges.

GROUP AND RE-GROUP

Feel free to play, rearrange, add to, or subtract from the work in progress, letting your thoughts diverge to create choices. For example, is there a relationship between the Grace Kelly show and the neo-conservative movement that might inspire a color mood? Can we find inspiration in the popularity of organic/sustainable food and fashion, and is the renewed interest in quilting and handicrafts part of the same movement? How will electronic music and its pop divas affect color trends? Will the oil spill in the Gulf of Mexico ignite a stronger interest in the environment? You will begin to observe color moods and themes and visualize how these might inspire a palette.

Sometimes the data converges like the pieces of a puzzle and we see the repetition of certain concepts and ideas clearly pointing the way to the season's trend and color direction. But trends can be contradictory, and often the more interesting concepts come from grouping things that at first glance do not belong together—for example tough with tender, urban with cowboys, or nature and technology. These contradictory concepts can often be successfully translated in a color palette, such as pastels accented with black, a synthetic bright popped in the middle of a neutral range, or earth tones mixed with metallics.

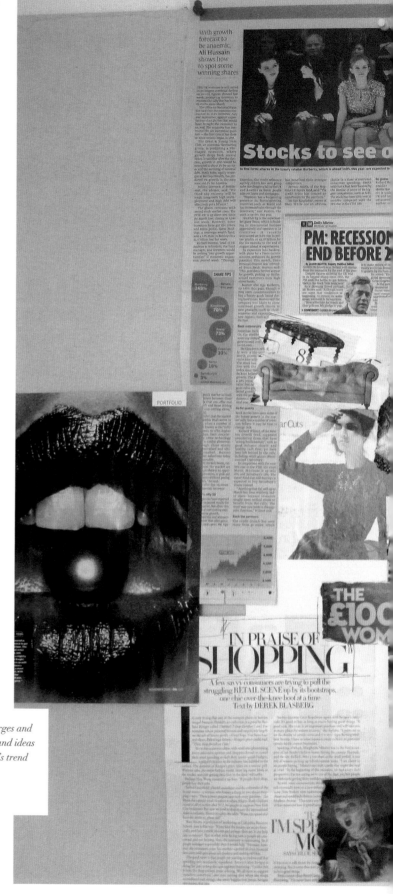

Sometimes the data converges and the repetition of concepts and ideas clearly point to the season's trend and color direction.

OBSERVE THE STANDALONE ELEMENTS

Sometimes contradictory trends can make us feel uncomfortable or unsure, or may include elements we find unappealing. But it is often these uncertain responses to out-of-context ideas that begin to evolve into something more stimulating. While our first goal is to understand the big picture, the observation or concept that stands alone and doesn't seem to fit should also be considered.

Martin Raymond points out that it is the individual, rather than the majority, who influences future trends. "Through watching and following and mapping the moves of the individual, the greater movement or cultural shift is made visible, not the other way around." (This is the individual identified as the "innovator" by Everett Rogers and Malcolm Gladwell, as noted in Chapter 4.)

The film director such as James Cameron who offers a vision of the future in 3D, the artist such as Banksy who refuses to deal with the commercial art world, the athlete who practices parcours rather than joining the football team, the young musician who plays jazz or folk rather than rap or pop are all examples of individuals who influence future trends. Our storyboards should contain innovative and contradictory concepts as well as more easily identifiable trends. By placing our inspirations and observations in the context of societal changes, we begin to draw meaning and suggestion from the storyboards. Eventually a story or theme will begin to emerge.

For example, an examination of politics in the Spring of 2010 would have found a sense in both the US and the UK that big government had become both expensive and intrusive, with a shift back to conservative values. There was a yearning for a return to local control and neighborhood organization. In an age of austerity, individuals were establishing micro-businesses that were local, pared-down, and less complex. Couple this with the movement toward local food and gardening, transparent sourcing, and sustainable raw materials, and you raise all sorts of questions about the hearts and minds of the consumers in the next two years—and what we might want to wear.

"Insight is the thing that will help you see where you need to go; knowledge is the fuel that ignites insight; information and data are the stepping stones that enable you to walk towards knowledge," Raymond writes.

Sometimes the image that is contradictory or stands alone points the way to a future trend.

BUILDING THE PALETTE

Once you feel strongly about the themes and color moods exhibited by your storyboards, begin to match colorful bits already collected, using Pantone or SCOTDIC textile swatches, or another standardized system. Then add additional colors to each grouping to build a palette. Play with a variety of shades and tones relating to the hues you have chosen.

It is possible that you may not find the exact shade you want; in this case some yarn, ribbon, fabric swatch, paper chips, or painted swatches may be used. Remember, however, that the color must eventually be matched and referenced by a color lab and dyer. Unusual materials and surfaces may prove difficult to match with accuracy and are best used as inspiration rather than the basis for actual colors.

The number of stories or groupings within your seasonal package will often depend on the nature of the project, as will the number of colors used in each group. Three or four groups is a good number for the beginning color forecaster, or if one is developing color for a specific project or product, but a professional may develop seven or eight groupings designed for different markets, end uses, or retail deliveries within an overall seasonal palette.

The number of stories or groupings within your seasonal package is variable; the number of colors within each group will vary as well.

Begin building your palette by matching colors already collected, then add additional colors to your grouping, using your knowledge of color theory, as well as your eye for what works.

The overall palette can be organized into groups of neutrals, pastels, brights, and deep or classic shades.

If broken up into groups, what story or inspiration will each group portray? Often a palette is organized into groups of neutrals, pastels, brights, and deep or classic shades. A more adventurous presentation may break the palette down into warm, cool, and achromatic groups. Practical considerations when developing a color palette include identifying the basic or core colors for the season, as well as accent shades and colors that are more directional.

You might build a group of contrasting brights in similar values; or you might build a range of cool or warm tonalities within a hue or color family (such as reds, greens, browns, etc.) and add a contrasting accent or two. You should probably include a classic story of basic shades, with cool or warm undertones according to the season and overall theme. For example, a palette of grays may be cool one season, or more taupe another; while blacks, reds, navies, and khakis can all have warm or cool undertones, or vary in value or intensity. As you build you may also edit or remove colors.

A classic story of basic shades should probably be included, with cool or warm undertones according to the season and current color cycle.

CROSS-CHECKING AGAINST LAST SEASON'S COLORS

This is the point where the color forecaster should cross-check the newly emerging palette against last season's palette and the larger color cycle. If one has researched current color at retail, observed the colors being worn and the colors left on the sales racks, and compared the designer runways with what is happening in the street, one should understand which hues and values are trending upward, and which are no longer fashion forward. Will the season be one of bright, bold color or monochromatic neutrals? Will colors be saturated, grayed, or whitened? Does the current zeitgeist call for gently transitioning from last season's palette? Or is a radical change in the air?

While a seasonal palette will likely contain a mix of hues, values, and intensities, there will generally be an overall mood or theme to the palette that reflects the current trend, and generally, the overall color cycle. A successful color will not be dropped from one season to the next, but may undergo a subtle modification at the hands of the color forecaster, designer, or merchandiser. For example, if warm colors have been strong in general, and a particular shade of blue-violet performed well last season, the color forecaster may tweak the color to a warmer, red-violet the next season.

It is important to understand that the development of a seasonal color palette is rarely a radical change, but more of an evolutionary process. The introduction of a new color or color family can take several seasons, and retailers and brands will often trial new colors in key test stores or markets in order to gauge consumer response. New colors are gradually filtered into consumer consciousness, so that by the time the color becomes established there is enough momentum for it to continue commercially.

Warm neutrals were well received for Spring/Summer 2010.

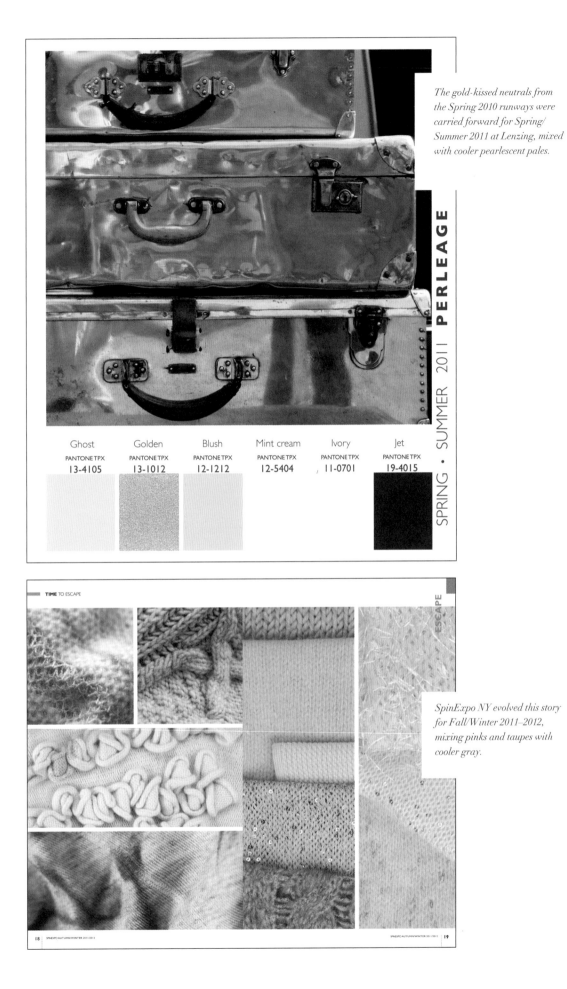

The gold-kissed neutrals from the Spring 2010 runways were carried forward for Spring/ Summer 2011 at Lenzing, mixed with cooler pearlescent pales.

SPRING · SUMMER 2011 | PERLEAGE

Ghost	Golden	Blush	Mint cream	Ivory	Jet
PANTONE TPX	PANTONE TPX	PANTONE TPX	PANTONE TPX	PANTONE TPX	PANTONE TPX
13-4105	13-1012	12-1212	12-5404	11-0701	19-4015

ESCAPE

SpinExpo NY evolved this story for Fall/Winter 2011–2012, mixing pinks and taupes with cooler gray.

A color story such as these
gold-cast neutrals becomes
established over several seasons;
it will eventually peak and then
decline in the classic bell curve as
discussed in Chapter 4.

Chloé moved into a pink-cast
taupe for Fall/Winter 2010, a
subtle modification of the previous
season's successful neutrals.

USING THE COLOR WHEEL AND COLOR THEORY

Here the forecaster's eye for color—based on a practiced taste level as well as a knowledge base of color theory and cycles—comes into play. There is no specific formula for choosing and grouping colors, but it does require experimentation with different combinations and proportions of color hue, chroma, and value. There are also decisions to be made regarding the structure of the overall palette, keeping in mind the end market, customer, or application. We will examine some of the differences in application in Chapter 6.

Playing with various combinations of three or four colors to assess the workability of the palette is also critical. Through an understanding of the color wheel and color theory, as well as drawing from one's memory or intuitive knowledge of "what works," the new color palette should offer a variety of options for combining the colors within each group as well as across groups in contrasts of intense colors with diluted ones, contrasts of warm and cool colors or combinations of closely related hues, complements of opposites or monochromatic mixes of related light to dark tones, or more sophisticated juxtapositions based on simultaneous contrast (see p.68).

The palette should be tested for workability by playing with various combinations of colors, using one's taste level and knowledge of color theory.

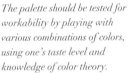

TESTING THE PALETTE

Try to picture these colors and combinations as solid, patterned, or printed garments. Will they match consumer's color needs: are they wearable, and will they complement what she has in her closet? Are they technically feasible: will they work in the season's desired fabrics? And are they a viable business strategy: are they saleable? Will they speak to the consumers' hearts and minds and meet a need that may or may not be articulated?

Many color forecasters will consult with trusted clients and colleagues to confirm the palette before it is finalized. Retail buyers and product development managers in particular may be consulted to get early "buy-in" and confirm the potential saleability of the proposed colors. At many trend bureaux, the palette may be initiated by a color specialist and then developed with a design team. In some cases the international agents working with the trend bureau are invited to view and discuss the almost-complete palette in light of their particular markets, as cultural perceptions of color can vary.

Try to picture your colors combined in stripes, checks, or patterns in various harmonies and contrasts, playing with values and cool or warm undertones.

Will the colors hang together attractively on the retail floor and appeal to the consumer?

Before the palette is finalized, many forecasters will consult with colleagues, clients, and retail buyers to confirm the potential saleability of the proposed colors.

FINAL PRESENTATION

The seasonal color package, usually purchased from the trend bureaux by subscription, will provide clients with the necessary tools to develop their products through a global supply chain. The package will generally include photos or other graphic representation of the season's major color themes.

Some forecasting services custom-dye yarn or fabric to their specifications; others will utilize ready-dyed Pantone, SCOTDIC, or other standardized references, which must be ordered in advance. In either case, the timeline to produce the published palette is short, and the colors of the palette will be put into work for reproduction as quickly as possible.

The colors may also be matched to a standard system for print or online publishing. The yarn reelings, pom-poms, or fabric swatches are then generally mounted on standard-sized cardstock in groups with appropriate visuals, color names, and copy, and packaged for distribution.

Unless the trend bureau is using a standardized color-matching service, they will generally offer additional yarn or fabric swatches for a nominal fee so that clients may send them to their suppliers for matching. Many professional color forecasters also provide suggested color combinations visualized through groupings of yarn or fabric swatches, or through specially designed yarn-dyed patterns.

Words are also an important and inspiring part of the forecasting package, and the color forecaster will usually prepare a written or verbal explanation of the colors and overall mood of the seasonal palette to reinforce the concept. Colors and groups may be given names, and careful consideration should be given to see that these translate across markets and cultures, as well as addressing the general spirit of the season. The color story may also address the suggested end uses and target markets of the colors and combinations. The subscription generally includes a group or personal consultation with the color forecaster, who will explain the season's color concepts and suggest end uses specific to the client(s).

The finalized presentation may feature a variety of inspirational materials or graphics in trend boards, much like an edited version of the working storyboard.

Commercial color services such as
LA Colors from Amsterdam may
offer their colors custom-dyed
into yarns or developed into
fabric swatches.

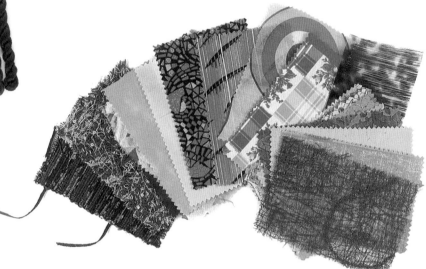

SPRING / SUMMER 2009
4 CLUB TROPICANA

Tropicana Curry
Tropicana Ochre
Tropicana Sun
Tropicana Orange
Tropicana Terra
Tropicana Rosso
Tropicana Purple
Tropicana Cocco

Forecasting services often provide
matching Pantone or SCOTDIC
references for the new seasonal
palette, as well as suggested
color combinations.

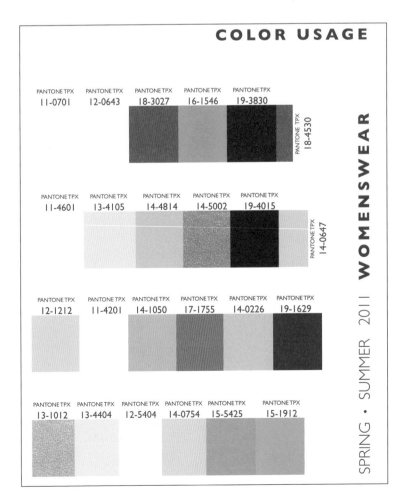

COLOR USAGE

PANTONE TPX	PANTONE TPX	PANTONE TPX	PANTONE TPX	PANTONE TPX	PANTONE TPX
11-0701	12-0643	18-3027	16-1546	19-3830	18-4530

PANTONE TPX	PANTONE TPX	PANTONE TPX	PANTONE TPX	PANTONE TPX	PANTONE TPX
11-4601	13-4105	14-4814	14-5002	19-4015	14-0647

PANTONE TPX	PANTONE TPX	PANTONE TPX	PANTONE TPX	PANTONE TPX	PANTONE TPX
12-1212	11-4201	14-1050	17-1755	14-0226	19-1629

PANTONE TPX	PANTONE TPX	PANTONE TPX	PANTONE TPX	PANTONE TPX	PANTONE TPX
13-1012	13-4404	12-5404	14-0754	15-5425	15-1912

SPRING • SUMMER 2011 **WOMENSWEAR**

TIMELINE OF A SEASON

With the economic downturn late in 2008 there was a pronounced change in the zeitgeist, which influenced color and fashion trends for 2010. An examination of the economic, social, and cultural trends of 2008 gives us some insight into the thought processes of color forecasters and designers and illustrates the linkage between the events of 2008 and fashion trends two years later.

While there were clearly many inspirations and observations that contributed to the individual color palettes developed for Spring/Summer 2010, by examining the colors in store for 2010 and thinking back through the cultural trends that influenced consumers we begin to understand how the forecaster approaches the building of a new palette.

Dow Jones experiences worst January in eight years

Hollywood writers' strike cancels Golden Globes and threatens Oscars—no red carpet glamour!

Buzzwords for 2008: Change. Bailout. Staycation. Twitter

War in Middle East enters eighth year. Uniforms, utilitarian, and camouflage are the main themes

The polar bear is declared an endangered species due to global warming

2008

JANUARY **FEBRUARY** **MARCH** **APRIL** **MAY** **JUNE**

Musician (and Karl Lagerfeld's fashion muse) Amy Winehouse wins five Grammy awards

Ready-to-wear collections for Fall/Winter 2008 shown at international Fashion Weeks; fabric fairs preview colors and fabrics for Spring 2009

Designers and forecasters travel, researching markets and gathering inspiration for Spring 2010 color direction

Takashi Murakami's show at Brooklyn Museum inspires childlike delight

Gas prices reach record highs; automative sales plummet

Intercolor delegates discuss brightness, luminosity, science, and chromatic experimentation for Spring 2010

British Textiles Colour Group palette for Spring 2010 includes nudes, sorbets, off-key brights, honey shades, tinted grays, lush greens, and blues

2008: Dow Jones experiences worst January in eight years.

Collapse of Lehman Brothers
in September pushes global
economy into meltdown

Fall fashion languishes on
store racks

Ready-to-wear collections
for Spring/Summer 2009
shown at international Fashion
Weeks; fabric fairs preview
colors and fabrics
for Fall 2009

Darwin exhibition opens in
London, anticipating
his 2009 bicentenary
and celebrating the colors
of nature

Obama elected first African-
American US president

Gothic and romantic revival:
Batman's *The Dark Knight* is
released, followed later in the
year by movie version
of *Twilight*

JULY　　**AUGUST**　　**SEPTEMBER**　　**OCTOBER**　　**NOVEMBER**　　**DECEMBER**

2008 Christmas sales
the worst in decades

Beijing hosts the Olympic
Games. It is the Asian decade

Slumdog Millionaire previews
at international film festivals;
its message—and colors—
make us feel good again

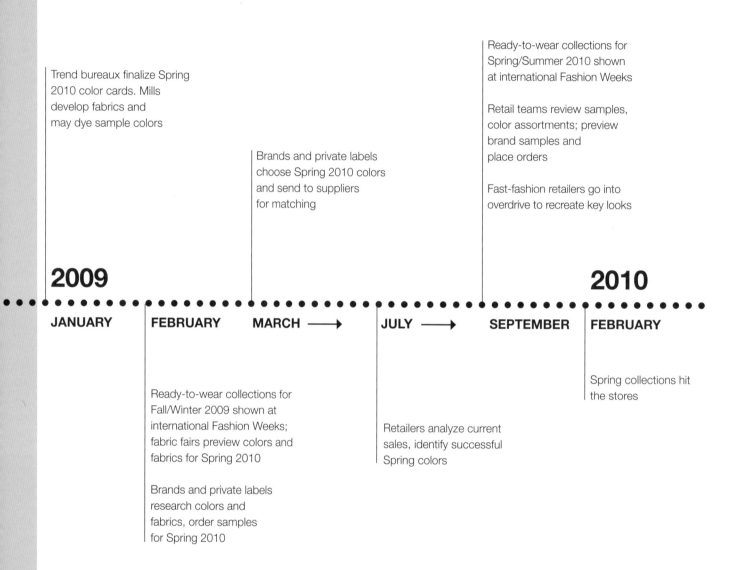

Trend bureaux finalize Spring 2010 color cards. Mills develop fabrics and may dye sample colors

Brands and private labels choose Spring 2010 colors and send to suppliers for matching

Ready-to-wear collections for Spring/Summer 2010 shown at international Fashion Weeks

Retail teams review samples, color assortments; preview brand samples and place orders

Fast-fashion retailers go into overdrive to recreate key looks

2009

2010

JANUARY   FEBRUARY   MARCH ⟶   JULY ⟶   SEPTEMBER   FEBRUARY

Ready-to-wear collections for Fall/Winter 2009 shown at international Fashion Weeks; fabric fairs preview colors and fabrics for Spring 2010

Brands and private labels research colors and fabrics, order samples for Spring 2010

Retailers analyze current sales, identify successful Spring colors

Spring collections hit the stores

SPRING 2010 COLLECTIONS REFLECT 2008'S EVENTS AND INSPIRATIONS

Reasons for good cheer— Murakami's cartoons, the movie Slumdog Millionaire, *Obama's election—and pretty spring brights at Philip Lim (below), Marc Jacobs, Stella McCartney, and others.*

In 2008 muse Amy Winehouse's look infused Lagerfeld's romantic fantasy with a darker undercurrent.

Exhibits for Darwin's bicentenary and growing concern for the environment inspired Alexander McQueen.

Playing it safe with utilitarianism—here at Chloé—was the reaction to the worst economic crisis in decades. With war and terrorism an everyday reality, military inspirations were also in evidence.

From China to India, the ascendency of Asian culture was bound to influence color and fashion, here from Dries Van Noten.

CHAPTER 6
COLOR APPLICATION

FROM THE COLOR FORECASTER TO THE RETAIL FLOOR

The process of researching, building, and distributing a fashion color palette is not the whole story. Color forecasters deliver a well-researched and carefully edited viewpoint to their customers—yarn and fabric dyers, print and pattern designers, brands, manufacturers, and retailers.

The next step in color development—actually putting colors into product—is as carefully thought-out as the building of the color forecast. No professional designer, brand manager, or retail merchandiser would simply take a color forecaster's palette and apply it to product without additional consideration of several factors. These include market positioning, target customer, classification, **retail assortments** (specifying the number of colors and percentage of each color within a range), and timing, as well as the actual end use and materials of the product itself.

The retail product developer's influence extends back through the brands and the suppliers of yarn, fabric, and components who provide product to their specifications. Large retailers such as Macy's, Bloomingdale's, Target, JC Penney, Kohl's, Saks, Harrods, John Lewis, and Debenhams now develop their own private label collections, which are contracted out to manufacturers, as well as stocking name brands each season.

In recent decades we have also seen the rise of **retail brands** that control the development, manufacturing, and logistics of their own product. These include chains such as Next, Zara, Mango, Topshop/Topman, Whistles, Jigsaw, Reiss, Banana Republic, Abercrombie & Fitch, J. Crew, Chico's, and American Apparel. "More and more, color work is being done in-house in retail, and designers will instruct the suppliers and manufacturers as to what colors they want," confirms UK color consultant Anna Starmer.

Depending on budget, retailers and brands will generally subscribe to three or four color forecast/trend services. Retail color and trend consultant Fran Yoshioka explains that in the US, "Online trend services have become a mainstay. Most large retailers subscribe to at least one large online service such as WGSN or Stylesight; one comprehensive domestic trend forecast service such as Doneger, and at least one color service such as Huepoint."

The professional color forecaster will hold consultations with these brand and retail decision makers to introduce and explain the palette, and in some cases may be retained by an important client to develop a "bespoke" presentation for a particular launch, department, or product development group. In addition, retailer and brand teams observe the runways and shop the fabric fairs and global retailers just as the color forecasters do, paying special attention to their direct competition.

Most retailers will adapt a forecaster's palette to suit their brand identity and target customer.

Spiced Riches

Color swatches prepared with Scotdic Colorspace.

Although these spice colors lend themselves to exotic interpretations, they can work equally well for contemporary sportswear. The richness of the colors suggests warmth. Newly favored velvets add to the mood.

Paisleys and eastern influence styling would work for a mainstream missy customer. This style direction could create great desk-to-dinner looks.

Contemporary and juniors could go for less traditional interpretations, such as leathers, and the new spice hues for velvets and velour. Could see these interpreted as ornate tops over jeans and boots. Balmain's runway worked into young, edgy interpretations of a rococo theme.

Who's Got The Look: Etro, Nanette Lepore, Balmain
Key Colors: Cinnamon, Saffron, Pomegranate, Teal, Berry Red
Accents: Brown, Terra Cotta, Ecru, Plum

SAFFRON GOLD
C-176007

PLUM
C-893510

TEAL
C-633005

SIENNA (RUST)
C-112504

BERRY RED
C-053512

WINE
C-012506

DARK BROWN
C-122001

CINNAMON SPICE
C-124010

How are colors ultimately chosen from the seasonal palette for consumer fashions, and who makes those decisions?

MAKING DECISIONS

While each retailer or brand has its own management and decision-making style, the choice of seasonal color for fashion product is very much a group decision. In the US, a creative director, fashion director, or trend manager is in charge of gathering and researching color and trends, and a designer or product development manager utilizes their recommendations in developing colors for a particular line or group. Someone from the business side, such as a merchandise manager or buyer, often has the final approval; and may seek confirmation further up the ladder from a general merchandise manager (GMM) or departmental merchandise manager (DMM).

According to Monsoon buyer Lia Williams in the UK, the specialty chain's range building is handled by designers and a colorist, with input from the buyer and merchandiser, who controls the budget and number of options per season. Similarly, at Arcadia (parent company for Topshop/Topman, Dorothy Perkins/Burton, and Miss Selfridge) the company's color specialist gathers the seasonal fabric color and trend information, then works with each of the designers and buyers on their particular ranges, each with its own brand identity.

A more detailed process is explained by Anna Starmer who consults with Marks & Spencer, which develops and stocks only in-house brands. "Days of work are taken planning which areas will use which colors. These are long, detailed meetings between designers, forecasters, and buyers to work out which colors best suit which garments, and then which color palettes should be in store in which month. Most retailers work with colors changing on a monthly basis, so there is a lot of weighing of options to make sure that there is choice for the customer between new drops."

"In M&S there are up to ten people all deciding the timing of colors. This is then presented to heads of buying and design, and often changed again; then presented to the director, who may change things again. Once the decisions are made, nothing is set in stone, as concept garments may not work in certain colors and we may have to rethink the whole thing! In a smaller company it can just be me and the head of design making these decisions, and if the color palettes look beautiful, then there will be little or no change throughout the process."

The retailer's design and buying teams analyze sales by color when creating the stories and colors for the coming season (or in the case of fast fashion, the next shipment), keeping in mind that if a color did not perform, it may simply be the wrong shade or cast of that color, or too early in the trend curve (see p.96) for the average customer. Within the volume market the commercial track record of a color will be carefully considered by the buying and merchandising teams in the development of their seasonal color palette.

PASSING OWNERSHIP OF THE PALETTE TO THE CLIENT

Because the retail approach to color development at the volume level relies to some extent on numbers, statistics, and post-sales analysis as well as on group consensus, some critics feel it does not speak to the real innovation needed in color and trend development. In some cases the retailer's approach may appear to diminish the importance of the color forecaster's role. Is something lost in the translation from the forecaster to the consumer?

"Trend forecasters provide general information—we have to use them as an influence and motivator, but the interpreter for a specific business, end use, or customer decides what becomes the trend," believes Fran Yoshioka. "I can give my opinions, and influence teams, but there is no guarantee that what I think is right will actually work on the final design/garment. I am employed to influence designers and buyers with my understanding of the colors that are on-trend," agrees Anna Starmer.

In a similar vein, UK textile and color consultant Beryl Gibson advises, "As a consultant designer you learn to give ownership of the project to the client. You facilitate the process going forward and share information. What I design has to go through manufacturing processes, yarn and fabric fairs but at the back of my mind there is always the customer. At the end of the day, it is about selling."

Retailer buyers and design teams analyze sales by color, and the commercial track record of a color is carefully considered in the development of the next color palette.

Retail brands are increasingly developing their own differentiated product by interpreting the color forecaster's direction for their specific target customer, resulting in a wider range of choices throughout the whole of the marketplace.

THE IMPACT OF RETAIL CLASSIFICATIONS AND DELIVERIES

With today's Internet access and social networking, color forecasters, designers, retailers, and consumers have unlimited access to much of the same information; anyone can download cultural, political, and economic data at warp speed. Observing the general zeitgeist, color forecasters may naturally develop seasonal stories that contain some of the same major concepts. This can occasionally lead to a situation where a single color or color mood can dominate the retail offerings in a season.

THE TARGET CUSTOMER

The dominance of a single color or color family allows the consumer fewer options for differentiation and can be a commercial disaster. While each color forecaster brings personal inspiration and individual flair to their seasonal palette, it is also important for the brand or retail decision-maker to work with the forecaster to interpret the season's key color directions appropriately and create a wide range of choices to suit a variety of target customers.

As brands and retailers increasingly develop their own differentiated product through internal design teams, understanding the target market and product end use is critical to the application of the forecaster's colors to a palette for a specific product. The suitability and applications of a hue or tone of color depend on a number of elements such as national or cultural preferences, function and price point of the product, and demographics of the target market.

Successful brands and retailers define their target customers by researching demographics and lifestyles, and through monitoring and analyzing sales data. Focus groups also help to reveal customer behaviors and decision-making processes, perceptions, and motivations. Using this information, retailers develop models or prototypes of their core customers. These prototypes vary by basic attributes such as gender, age, size, price point, as well as by education, interests, marital and family status, and where the customer falls on Nystrom's innovation curve (innovators, early adopters, and so on, see p.96).

Product developers and merchandisers must have a firm understanding of their market or target customer, based on this market research, and know how to interpret the forecaster's information to create saleable product specifically for that customer. "This takes a highly skilled person that understands the ultimate end use of color and trend information, what it must accomplish in product, and how to visualize its effect," according to Fran Yoshioka.

APPAREL CATEGORIES

While brands target different consumer types, they also fall within apparel categories or **retail classifications**, which differ from country to country. In Europe there are categories such as outerwear, tailored clothing, career wear, leisure wear, knitwear, dresses, evening wear, holiday wear, and sportswear; while in the US the equivalent classifications might be outerwear, suits and career separates, uniforms, sportswear, sweaters, day dresses, after-five, beach or cruise, and activewear.

In the US, women's apparel in the larger department stores is also differentiated by lifestyle/price point classifications. Most expensive and sophisticated, of course, is couture and designer, followed by bridge (often career-oriented), contemporary (a more youthful attitude and slimmer cut), missy (classic in attitude with a less body-conscious fit), moderate, and budget. More and more retailers, small and large, choose to dedicate themselves to one of these classifications; for example, JC Penney focuses on the moderate customer, Wal-Mart on the budget customer, and Neiman Marcus on the couture through contemporary customer. While these classifications do not exist per se in the UK and Europe, there is certainly a similar sense of departmental segmentation in department stores such as John Lewis, Selfridges, Galeries Lafayette, Printemps, La Rinascente, and El Corte Inglés.

The colors appropriate for various fashion products at a particular retailer within a given season, then, will differ from one department to the next. For example, a particular bright red hue could be overkill worked as a solid in tailored clothing for the office, but would be entirely appropriate for an after-five dress or a top for the gym, and might look fashion-forward in a coat.

Large retailers and brands with global distribution will also consider regional differences in climate, population, cultural preferences, and lifestyle when assigning the colors for a particular line or classification. This is especially important for Western brands hoping to succeed in the emerging markets of Asia and the Middle East, and color trends must be confirmed with local marketing research.

TIMING

The application of color in fashion products is further complicated by the number of deliveries of fresh merchandise within a season. In the US, retailers generally deliver new merchandise, or a new assortment of color for a core basic, every two months in the womenswear or "missy" category, according to Fran Yoshioka. Bestselling fashion colors, for example purple, will be repeated or updated from season to season until they are past-peak; at some point the consumer will have a closet-full and the color is said to have "over-performed." In the fast-fashion arena, the changeover is much more rapid, with new merchandise arriving weekly.

Deciding when to place new color on the retail floor, when to commit to the color in depth, and when to move a color to the markdown rack can make a great deal of difference to the success or failure of a collection or retail season. If the color is introduced too early—before consumers are ready to accept it—it may not sell. If the color is introduced too late, the market may be oversaturated or in its post-peak phase. A brand or retailer introducing a color that is already on the sale racks elsewhere will likely experience poor sell-through.

Many retailers report that 70 percent of garments are sold in the basic colors such as black, gray, navy, khaki, and white. (The truth of this percentage depends on the garment, the department, and the target market; a high-end fashion range or collection will likely use a higher percentage of forward color.) According to retail merchandising director Elaine M. Flowers, "Say you have a basic T-shirt and plan to run it all season. You might start out with eight colors, four of which would be your basics through the season (black, navy, white or ecru, red) and then do four fashion colors for each delivery. You could also change the cast of basics such as navy or red."

At Monsoon, three or four new ranges are launched each month, including a fast-fashion range known as "Fusion," according to Lia Williams. The palette for each story would be between seven to ten colors including highlight or accent colors for linings and print combinations. A large retailer with numerous in-house brands such as Marks & Spencer may employ as many as 200 colors four times a year. On the other hand, fast-fashion brands such as Zara, Topshop, and Forever 21 will bring in new trend-right merchandise on a weekly or twice-weekly basis, utilizing the most forward colors based on runway trends, customer feedback, and sales data.

Design and color consultant Sandy McLennan likens this complex process of assigning trend-right, saleable color to various retail classifications and deliveries to playing "color Sudoku—where you backfit and rationalize your initial thoughts to suit categories and assortments."

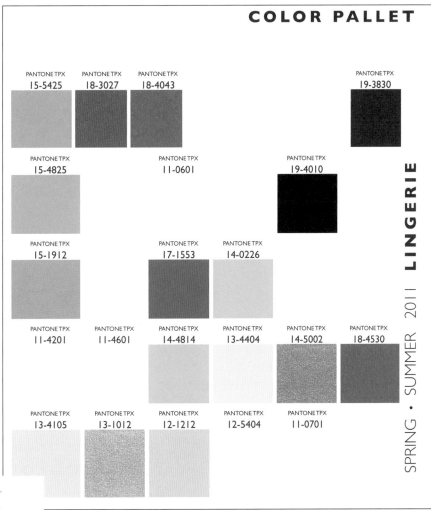

COLOR PALLET

PANTONE TPX	PANTONE TPX	PANTONE TPX
15-5425	18-3027	18-4043

PANTONE TPX	PANTONE TPX
15-4825	11-0601

PANTONE TPX
19-3830

PANTONE TPX
19-4010

PANTONE TPX	PANTONE TPX	PANTONE TPX
15-1912	17-1553	14-0226

PANTONE TPX	PANTONE TPX	PANTONE TPX	PANTONE TPX	PANTONE TPX	PANTONE TPX
11-4201	11-4601	14-4814	13-4404	14-5002	18-4530

PANTONE TPX	PANTONE TPX	PANTONE TPX	PANTONE TPX	PANTONE TPX
13-4105	13-1012	12-1212	12-5404	11-0701

SPRING · SUMMER 2011 **LINGERIE**

Color application differs by apparel category, although intimate apparel, or lingerie, is increasingly influenced by ready-to-wear colors.

Even categories such as hosiery have their own palette, carefully composed to complement the season's dominant color themes.

MEN, WOMEN, AND CHILDREN

Color diversity and experimentation is greatest in the women's fashion business, as women spend more on apparel. In general, the higher the price point, the more sophisticated the colorway. While high-end fashion tends to include black, gray, and offbeat neutrals such as taupe or brown in order to highlight more intricate or artisanal fabric, cut, and ornamentation, some designers may utilize a carefully considered color palette with eye-catching or more forward colors and unusual color combinations.

Fashion colors for menswear, of course, are different than those applied to womenswear, although both will relate to the season's dominant color families. Elaine M. Flowers tells us that, "menswear tends to always rely on a strong set of seasonal basics for bottoms but brings in fashion newness in knitwear and shirtings." T-shirts, ties, hosiery, sneakers, and seasonal leisure or beachwear for men usually incorporate the season's more fashion-forward colors; one example would be the appearance of colorful suede driving mocs for men from the likes of Tod's, Kurt Geiger, and Paul Smith in Spring 2010.

Categories such as childrenswear and intimate apparel also rely on seasonal color direction within the parameters of the product. Children's clothing tends to utilize clear, cheerful basics and brights (although the category is increasingly trend-oriented due to the influence of "tweens," fashion-savvy pre-teenagers), while intimate apparel is driven by skin tones as well as fashion shades and traditional "feminine" hues such as pink and red.

In general, mid-market brands and retailers will utilize "safe" colors, combined with more fashionable colors at the peak of their popularity. UK color consultant Sue Chorley Fish explains that "for middle market brands often the same key colors sell time and time again, and the safer customer looks to the brand to keep providing dependable basics."

While menswear relies on basics such as black, gray, navy, and tan, seasonal colors for men's accessories incorporate more fashion-forward colors.

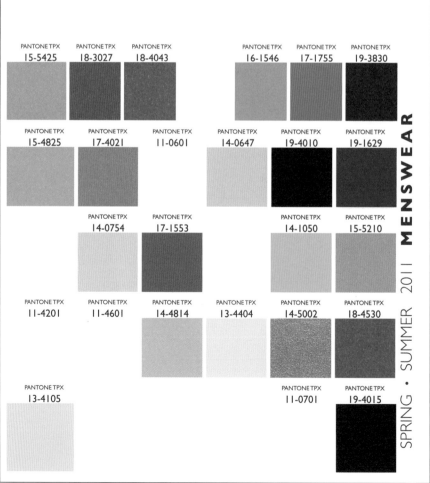

COLOR PALLET

MENSWEAR

SPRING · SUMMER 2011

PANTONE TPX 15-5425	PANTONE TPX 18-3027	PANTONE TPX 18-4043		PANTONE TPX 16-1546	PANTONE TPX 17-1755	PANTONE TPX 19-3830
PANTONE TPX 15-4825	PANTONE TPX 17-4021	PANTONE TPX 11-0601	PANTONE TPX 14-0647	PANTONE TPX 19-4010	PANTONE TPX 19-1629
	PANTONE TPX 14-0754	PANTONE TPX 17-1553		PANTONE TPX 14-1050	PANTONE TPX 15-5210
PANTONE TPX 11-4201	PANTONE TPX 11-4601	PANTONE TPX 14-4814	PANTONE TPX 13-4404	PANTONE TPX 14-5002	PANTONE TPX 18-4530
PANTONE TPX 13-4105				PANTONE TPX 11-0701	PANTONE TPX 19-4015

COLOR PALLET

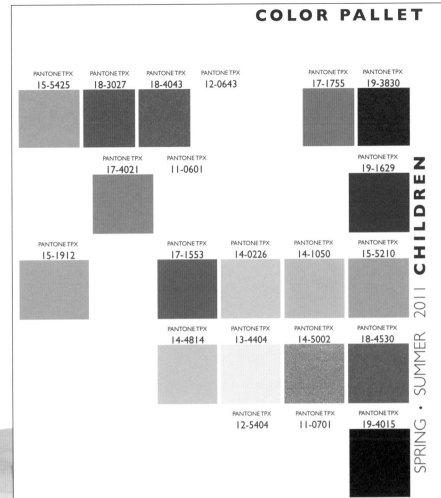

PANTONE TPX 15-5425	PANTONE TPX 18-3027	PANTONE TPX 18-4043	PANTONE TPX 12-0643
PANTONE TPX 17-4021	PANTONE TPX 11-0601
PANTONE TPX 15-1912	PANTONE TPX 17-1553	PANTONE TPX 14-0226	PANTONE TPX 14-1050	PANTONE TPX 15-5210
PANTONE TPX 14-4814	PANTONE TPX 13-4404	PANTONE TPX 14-5002	PANTONE TPX 18-4530
PANTONE TPX 12-5404	PANTONE TPX 11-0701	PANTONE TPX 19-4015
PANTONE TPX 17-1755	PANTONE TPX 19-3830
PANTONE TPX 19-1629

SPRING · SUMMER 2011 CHILDREN

Children's clothing tends to utilize clear, cheerful basics and brights, but is becoming ever more sophisticated.

COLOR IN VISUAL MERCHANDISING

Based on the overall color and trend direction for the season, retail merchandisers and product development teams not only develop individual palettes for each department, category, and delivery within the store, but will adhere to an overall or strategic color theme for **visual merchandising,** advertising, etc. Visual merchandising is the way product is displayed in store—in windows, on mannequins, and grouped in racks, rounders, or shelves in a department.

Store windows such as those at Selfridges in London and Barneys in New York have become an elaborate, expensive, and effective means of projecting a store's image, and color plays an important part in the creation of store windows, within the overall seasonal theme or message. Visual merchandising is generally led by a creative department or strong creative director such as Barneys' Simon Doonan, Selfridges' Alannah Weston, or (until recently) Liberty's Tamara Salman.

Whether the featured garments are from the store's own brand or an assortment of name brands, they will work together in various color contrasts or harmonies to create a cohesive message much like the colors in a forecaster's palette. Strategic color statements provide variety in terms of visual merchandising, and choice for the consumer within the continuity and evolution of the trend throughout the season.

Grouping product by color story, rather than by manufacturer or size, is another form of visual merchandising that will get the seasonal color message across. The goal is to show how the product can work in a number of different ways and to encourage the customer to purchase several products to recreate the look in a range of colors.

Monsoon's Lia Williams calls visual merchandising "massively influential. The product could be amazing but the customer needs to know the product is in store." Sue Chorley Fish confirms that visual merchandising is essential in a world where the consumer is surrounded by sophisticated visual stimuli—"It brings to life the story that the brand needs to tell the consumer—communicating the look, the mood, the spirit." For some retail brands such as Zara, Mango, or Anthropologie, visual merchandising often proves more effective than advertising.

Visual merchandising and marketing also include print advertising, Internet sites, catalogs, and artistic fashion "magalogues" or "catazines" (a combination of catalog and magazine) seen at brands/retailers such as Abercrombie & Fitch, Neiman Marcus, Harvey Nichols, Mango, Galeries Lafayette, Toast, and Triumph Motorcycle, to name a few; these catazines are increasingly found on the Internet. In addition, the use of color in logos, hang tags, shopping bags, and even tissue wrapping all contribute to the consumer's perception of the brand and product.

A successful visual merchandising campaign will inspire the consumer to purchase, with the store window display as the showcase that invites one to step inside.

Mannequins drive multiple sales by showing the customer how the garments look in a three-dimensional view, as well as demonstrating how to put outfits together, including accessories.

Visual merchandising also includes print catalogs and websites that can convey a strong color message.

TOAST

high summer 2006

COLOR IN CONTEXT

Although the color of a product is the first thing that we see, a single color does not work independently but must be viewed in the context of the particular product, its end use, and how it is to be worn. The physical setting of a color, the store lighting, the fabric texture, the product's shape and substrate, or material from which it is made, will all influence the color's aesthetic and commercial appeal.

Many elements are factored into the designer's choice of color for a fashion item: the product's size and shape, potential longevity and fashion relevance, and what the choice of color says about the target consumer. Color strength and tonal value can alter the appearance of a garment. A color that is flattering to the wearer can positively transform how the wearer behaves and is perceived by others. "The best color in the whole world, is the one that looks good, on you!" claimed Coco Chanel.

The use of color in printed, knitted, and yarn-dyed combinations or solid ensembles also relies on context. As we have seen, the perception of color is altered by the colors that surround it and the proportion of each. The dominant, or largest area of color in a combination will suggest a mood, while the subordinate or accent shades might harmonize or be discordant with this.

When developing the overall palette or suggesting color combinations for textiles or apparel, the color forecaster must keep the proportion of cool and warm colors in mind. Cool colors appear to have less weight and tend to reduce the size of an object, in comparison with the warmer hues.

Likewise, color value—the whiteness or darkness of a color—must be considered in proportion. Darker shades will seem to reduce size, whereas lighter or brighter colors will be perceived as larger. It has become traditional to use darker colors for apparel on the lower part of the body, with warmer or brighter colors used near the face.

As we have seen, social and cultural context influence the end use of color. Colors may be considered masculine or feminine; a particular hue may be appropriate in one social setting but not in another. Using color in an unexpected context can make it look fresh and new, a technique cleverly employed by Sir Paul Smith in items such as a pink corduroy suit, a purple lining, or a blue cuff on a green shirt. "Simply changing the color or texture of something quite normal turns it into something completely new," he advises.

The alteration of one or two color elements in a pattern can influence our perception of the garment, making it appropriate for one target customer or classification rather than another. Picture a romantic floral pattern colored in sophisticated neutrals rather than typical floral shades; or a traditional plaid or tweed traced with lime green or purple.

Using color in an unexpected context can make it fresh and new, as in Paul Smith's use of "feminine" pink in a very "masculine" suit.

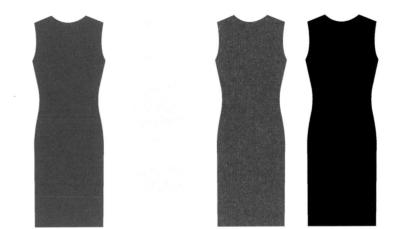

Warm colors and brighter values such as red and yellow tend to increase the perceived size of the body, while cool and darker colors such as blue and black create the opposite effect.

If re-colored in sophisticated neutrals, this romantic floral would appeal to a very different customer base.

LIMITATIONS IN COLOR APPLICATIONS

The application of color can sometimes be limited by the fabric or materials used, as some colors will not dye satisfactorily in certain fibers or substrates. For example, cotton is not easily saturated and can appear a bit dull in high shades. A brightly colored cotton garment trimmed in a dyed-to-match silk or viscose will never look quite as saturated as the trim fabric. In addition, the costs of some dyestuffs used to achieve highly saturated shades can be expensive, making them sometimes inappropriate for lower-priced product.

Oil-based synthetics (polyester and nylon) and microfibers have a similar problem, and color fastness can be an issue, especially when combined with spandex products. This is particularly critical in activewear, swimwear, and intimate apparel, where garments are subject to frequent washing or exposure to chlorine or salt water. Specifying white trim for a red or black garment in a polyester/spandex fabric is a recipe for disaster (unless the trim is made from a substrate that does not absorb the same dyestuffs used on the polyester.)

Pure whites are difficult to achieve in animal products such as wool, silk, and leather. This means a wool scarf, sweater, or leather bag dyed to match a white garment in cotton will be a disappointment; better to match the garment to the white achievable on the more difficult substrate.

The color limitations of various materials, then, are an important consideration when matching trims and findings, or when a garment is pieced from different fabrics in the same color. Intimate apparel, with its many different fabrics and components, is a good example. Color forecasters and decision makers should have a basic understanding of fibers and fabrics in order to manage expectations.

Environmental concerns have also begun to alter the colors achievable on some substrates, as certain dyestuffs and saturation levels result in unsafe effluents. While most dyers in the West have refined their processes and reduced pollution, and chemical companies are developing less harmful dyestuffs, textile production in Asia and Africa continues to pollute vast stretches of waterways. The movement into sustainable sourcing provides a social context that may alter color preferences for a particular line or product, resulting in the application of more subtle colors and natural dyestuffs, and the use of recycled fibers and fabrics that may be more difficult to dye.

Colorfastness is critical in end uses such as swimwear and activewear, but can be difficult to achieve in high shades in fabrics made of synthetics and spandex.

The color limitations of various materials can affect the matching of myriad components utilized in a product such as intimate apparel.

BEYOND APPAREL: THE INFLUENCE OF COLOR TRENDS

The reach of the color forecaster's palette goes beyond fashion apparel, crossing over into accessories and cosmetics, and influencing other fields from automobiles and products for the home to corporate communications and packaging. The recent use of bright or metallic colors in designer bags, belts, and shoes has done much to rejuvenate sales of leather goods. Costume jewelry also reflects color trends—some seasons will see the dominance of a material such as gold or silver, or a particular colored stone, such as turquoise, coral, amber, or jet.

Cosmetics in particular are strongly linked with the colors seen in fashion apparel. Makeup artists create seasonal signature looks for the runways to complement designers' clothing and vision. Recent Fashion Weeks have brought us lip and nail colors ranging from nude to black to pale pink to orange and most recently peach, lilac, and gray, with eye shadow in metallic greens, blues, bronzes, and 1980s-inspired neons.

Bright color has helped to rejuvenate sales of accessories such as bags and shoes.

The major cosmetic companies may consult with color forecasters in developing seasonal color ranges, and issue seasonal cosmetic ranges with interesting themes and color names that relate to current fashion trends. For Spring 2010 Esteé Lauder teamed with Michael Kors for a line of hot Hollywood colors, while MAC launched four separate "Color Forecast" palettes, and Chanel's colors were clean and neutral in honor of Coco Chanel's legacy.

Nail color has become an important fashion color category over the past decade, with nail specialists such as OPI, Jessica, and Essie competing with trendier brands such as Rococo, China Glaze, Zoya, and Butter London, as well as the more established cosmetics brands. OPI in particular reflects current culture in its choice of color themes and names, with Spring 2010 offers including "Alice in Wonderland" and the "Hong Kong Collection."

While color forecasting's applications lie first and foremost in fashion, when it comes to color the term "fashion" is growing to include a wide array of consumer and corporate products.

Fashion cosmetics are strongly linked with the colors seen in fashion apparel; nail color has become a particularly important category.

The soft pink lighting in the Beauty Bar's cosmetics display illustrates the use of color in visual marketing.

Costume jewelry is an important accessory that will reflect current color trends in apparel.

WHAT DOES THE CONSUMER REALLY WANT?

The retailer's focus is on giving the consumer what he or she wants. A great deal of time and money is spent on developing the profile of that customer, who may be referred to as "the guest" (at Target) or the capitalized designation SHE (at Chico's), or even by a name chosen to represent a particular demographic (Marias, Janes, or Heathers, for example).

Retail and brand decision makers analyze colors in terms of sales figures and consumer response before applying the forecaster's recommendation to product. Certain colors with a history of poor performance with a retailer's target customer—say, for example, lime green among career women—are not likely to be accepted by the retail buyer or merchandiser, even if the color forecaster believes strongly in lime green that season.

Ultimately, how do we determine what the consumer really wants, if they can only choose from what is offered? A recent article by Dr. Tracy Diane Cassidy of Manchester Metropolitan University claims that while color forecasters aim for 80 percent accuracy in anticipating consumer color preferences, consumer surveys show the success rate to be 51 percent. Cassidy proposes the use of a personal color analysis system as a model for a color preference data collection system to assist the color forecasting and development process.

Personal color analysis systems such as Color Me Beautiful and Angela Wright's *The Beginner's Guide to Colour Psychology* became popular in the 1980s and generally involve assigning one of four seasonal palettes to a consumer, based on questionnaire responses including skin tone, eye color, and hair color. The palette is supposed to predict the consumer's color preferences in terms of hue, saturation, and value.

However, Cassidy's survey showed that most consumers favored colors from a number of palettes, with few consumers having strong preferences for only one palette and even then not liking all colors within that palette. Thus the success rate of color prediction from the personal analysis method was no better than the current forecasting method.

Color forecasters offer an aesthetic, relevant, and thematic insight into newness, grounded in the observation, research, and analysis of current culture. Properly applied, the current process of color forecasting remains the best option for providing a wide range of saleable product through color that is fresh, appealing, and wearable—giving the consumer a reason to buy.

The goal of color forecasting is to determine what consumers really want to buy, and to provide them with the products and motivation to do so.

CHAPTER 7
INTUITION AND
INSPIRATION IN
COLOR FORECASTING

Displays at trade shows may stimulate our "right brain" or emotional intelligence to imagine how the colours might relate to other observations or images in our memory, thus allowing new concepts to develop.

WHAT DRIVES THE CREATIVE PROCESS?

While it is important to understand color theory, the historical and cultural uses of color, and the cyclical nature of trends, most theorists will acknowledge that there is also a creative element in color forecasting that cannot necessarily be taught in a classroom. The forecaster must be observant and open to the inspirational ways in which color is used in the world around them, and then must combine that inspiration with research, observation, and experience to develop an acceptable commercial palette.

Innovation as the result of the creative process in color forecasting or fashion design can change the course of a fashion cycle, alter consumer buying patterns, and in the best cases drive sales. Originality is what makes an artist or fashion designer truly unique—Van Gogh or Gauguin or Picasso, Poiret or Saint Laurent or McQueen. True creators don't always pay attention to consumer trends or fashion cycles, but seem to explode with ideas and new products.

In reality, creativity is driven both by inspiration, or *exterior* stimulation; and by intuition, an *interior* insight or perception that is independent of any reasoning process. Inspiration and intuition work hand-in-hand and can be operating at the same time. They are known as **right-brain** skills; rather than recording and measuring quantitative data—facts and figures—they deal with emotional intelligence, the ability to know something in one's gut, to believe in the heart rather than in the brain.

While the color forecaster can observe and record measurable data such as sales figures, trend curves, and visitors to social networks, it is much more difficult to measure the significance of a piece of art, a wonder of nature, a new exhibition, or a political movement. In *The Trendmaster's Guide* Robyn Waters reminds us, "Keep in mind that all analyses measure results only *after* something has already happened… if it weren't for visionaries who knew how to *go with their instincts* we'd be living in a world without Post-it notes, FedEx, and Starbucks double tall skim lattes."

The forecaster must pay attention to inspiration and intuition as well as to cycles and buying patterns. "Make it a habit to notice, really notice what *takes your breath away,* stimulates your senses, ignites your passions, inspires awe, and delivers delight," writes Waters. Inspiration and intuition can refresh the thought process with new ideas, visions, and concepts.

Many creative concepts spring from an intuitive or inspirational moment.

A visual image of tie-dyeing may not only serve as color inspiration, but also stimulate cultural references which may multiply into a kaleidoscope of ideas and concepts.

Trend identification comes from using our radar to tap into the world around us.

INSPIRATION IS EVERYWHERE

For many designers and forecasters, the first instinct when seeking inspiration for a new season is to veer in the opposite direction from the previous one. Pat Tunsky asks herself: "How can I develop the next season to look new and different and *inspirational* to our clients?" Design consultant Joanna Bowring comments, "Each season starts afresh and positive, mostly, though there is an element of reacting, looking for the new/opposite of what has just happened."

Designer Marc Jacobs, interviewed in 2009 at *Women's Wear Daily's* CEO summit, acknowledged the randomness of inspiration, especially at the beginning of a new season. "For me, it starts in this really arbitrary fashion… we just did this, so let's do something completely different."

Inspiration stimulates the senses and the imagination in a powerful and emotional way. It comes from observing our external world—the arts, nature, architecture, geography, travel, food, sport, music, or celebrities—almost any part of the culture. UK color consultant Sue Chorley Fish writes, "Trend identification comes from soaking up the world around you and looking to those creatives who ignite, inspire, and breathe newness. Newness can come from any field."

In *Inspiring Writing in Art and Design*, author and lecturer Pat Francis comments on the issue of creativity and inspiration. "The processes of creativity involve a collecting and sifting and sorting of information, both at first and second hand, using both primary and secondary research. But research can also be about practice—therefore what is being encouraged is the active experimentation and practice of work: researching how a line varies, how colors collide or collude, and this may then lead to research into artists who explored in similar ways…."

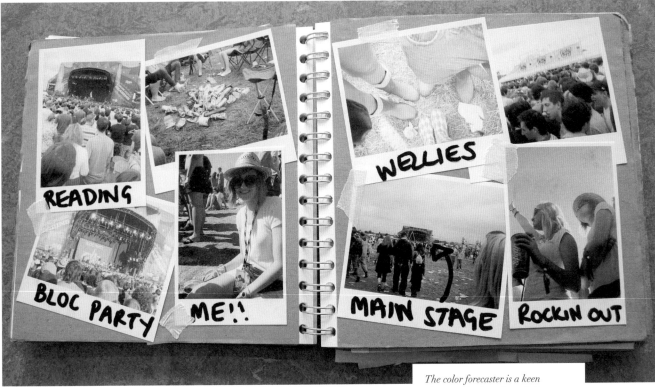

The color forecaster is a keen observer of culture from high to low, visiting a wide variety of venues wherever people mingle and exchange ideas.

CULTURE, TRAVEL, AND NATURE

According to trendmaster Robyn Waters, "Trend trackers and creative types tend to be very curious people. We exhibit a voracious appetite for knowledge." Visiting a wide variety of venues where people congregate, mingle, and exchange ideas— galleries, museums, movie houses, theaters, music festivals, clubs, vintage stores, crafts markets, urban neighborhoods, sporting events, and trade fairs—the forecaster hones a skill we can best describe as a "radar" or "antennae" to tap into what is different, new, important.

Travel will expand our color repertoire with new and unfamiliar cultural references. Roseann Forde of Fordecasting in New York finds inspiration in travel and the physical world of nature: "… the brilliant orange blossoms in Jamaica, the aqua water in the Bahamas, and the faded building façades of southern Europe."

Likewise, the natural world will provide unceasing color inspiration, from the four seasons to the blue-green oceans, the pink sand deserts, the snow-dusted mountains, and emerald rain forests. Flora and fauna display all the colors of the rainbow and beyond. Gardens and flowers are rich sources of inspiration.

The artwork, artifacts, and costumes of other cultures offer bountiful inspiration.

The natural world will provide unceasing color inspiration.

Travel is essential in the research of color and fashion inspiration.

Many color forecasters and designers find gardens and flowers particularly inspirational.

MAGAZINES

Forde also cites the use of beautifully photographed lifestyle magazines such as *Bloom* and *Côté Sud*. Other inspirational magazines include *Crafts*, *Selvedge*, *Viewpoint*, *Textile View*, *Architectural Digest*, *Dwell*, and the various international editions of *Vogue*, just to name a few. Independent magazines such as *i-D*, *Dazed & Confused*, *Another Magazine*, *Another Man*, *Pop*, *Love*, *Tank*, *Wallpaper**, *Intelligent Life*, and *10 & 10 Man* are well produced and shed light on cultural movements of the moment.

Following the demise of several traditional titles during the 2009 recession, a number of new and independent style and culture magazines have recently launched. Titles such as *Twin*, *Glass*, *Perfect*, and *Gray* offer limited and expensive editions that are more like coffee table books than magazines. They provide an alternative to the rapidly expanding world of fashion blogs and online publications, which may also provide inspiration. (There is a list of some of these websites on p.186.)

An array of design magazines provides a wealth of inspiring images and concepts.

ART AND DESIGN

Historical art and design movements have frequently inspired color trends in fashion apparel, particularly when an artist or designer is the subject of a major exhibition, book, or movie. Recent influential design exhibitions include Vionnet at the Les Arts Décoratifs, Musée de la Mode in Paris, and the 2010 Saint Laurent retrospective at the Petit Palais.

Musuem exhibitions such as Grace Kelly at London's Victoria & Albert Museum and the American Style show at the Metropolitan Museum of Art in New York reawakened an interest in American designs of the first half of the twentieth century. We have seen how the exotic colors of the Ballet Russes inspired designers from Poiret to YSL to Galliano; the V&A's 2010/2011 Ballet Russes exhibition will likely usher in a resurgence of exotic design.

Mondrian's geometric paintings influenced Yves Saint Laurent's collection in 1965, and Mark Rothko's sober colors were borrowed by several American designers in 2006. The artist Gustav Klimt's "golden phase" palette inspired *Vogue Italia's* remarkable December 2007 spread (styled by Edward Enninful and shot by Steven Meisel) and Galliano's Spring 2008 couture collection for Dior; Klimt's use of metallics and jewel tones has also influenced Prada and most recently Make Up For Ever's gold-kissed makeup palette.

Today we have graffiti-inspired fashion in the successful collaboration of artist/designer Stephen Sprouse with Marc Jacobs for Louis Vuitton, and in graphic T's featuring the artwork of Basquiat and Banksy.

Beyond art books and museums, vintage stores, old magazines, and flea markets are all excellent sources for historical color inspiration.

Colors from the arts have inspired designers over the years, from the Ballet Russes (Poiret) to Mondrian (Saint Laurent) to Klimt (Galliano) and Stephen Sprouse (Marc Jacobs.)

Today we find graffiti-inspired fashion in designer collaborations and mass-produced T-shirts.

MUSES

Many creators (artists, writers, musicians) are inspired by a personal **muse**. Contemporary examples include Picasso with Dora Maar, Andy Warhol with Edie Sedgwick, Lewis Carroll with Alice Liddell, John Lennon with Yoko Ono, Yves Saint Laurent with Loulou de la Falaise, Gianni Versace with his sister Donatella, and Marc Jacobs with Sofia Coppola. Some designers, such as Karl Lagerfeld, change muses with practically every collection; Lagerfeld has been inspired by muses as diverse as Inès de la Fressange, Claudia Schiffer, and Amy Winehouse.

In contemporary culture, celebrities have become muses and style icons, inspiring color and fashion trends in their own right. Today's muses include models such as Kate Moss and Agyness Deyn; political wives such as Michelle Obama and Carla Bruni; actresses like Sarah Jessica Parker, the Olsen twins, and Emma Watson; and royalty such as Queen Rania of Jordan and Princess Letizia of Asturias. Editors, stylists, and photographers who work closely with the fashion community also inspire designers and consumers alike with their creativity and eye for detail.

Many creators are linked with a personal muse, or inspirational "goddess," a tradition that comes from classical mythology, where nine sister goddesses presided over the arts.

CONTEMPORARY DESIGNERS AND RETAILERS

The color statements of contemporary designers and retailers each season not only take inspiration from everywhere but often serve in turn as inspiration for fast fashion and the mass market. For Spring 2010 we saw Dries Van Noten turn to the increasingly powerful China and Southeast Asia for his signature culturally inspired textiles in a range of earthy deeps and brights such as ocher, indigo, mustard, and cinnabar.

In the same season, Karl Lagerfeld's fresh floral colors and delicate tea-stained pastels at Chanel provided a welcome escape from the financial crisis. While the two looks were very different, both quite cannily resonated with the political, economic, and social ideas of the day, and inspired color palettes that were quickly interpreted by the chain stores such as Zara, Topshop, and New Look.

Marc Jacobs' collection for Fall/Winter 2010 was built on beautiful classics in a palette of camel, gray, and taupe. The collection spoke brilliantly to an era of uncertainty with timeless and elegant colors that made consumers feel confident they were purchasing something enduring and of value. Jacobs presaged the Grace Kelly and American Style exhibitions, capturing a shift in the zeitgeist to a more conservative look that influenced mass-market shoppers as well.

Color forecasters are shoppers—of retail trends as well as of culture and design movements. Comparative and competitive retail research, from flea market stalls and vintage specialists to crafts fairs, niche markets, and chain stores, is a rich source of stimulation.

In the 1980s two very different retailers, Muji from Japan and Ikea from Sweden, became successful with a simple, functional approach to products for the home and, in Muji's case, both home and apparel. These well-designed basics were simple, clean, and monochromatic, accented with cheerful splashes of color. This "utilitarian" concept—good design made affordable to everyone—transitioned to other retailers such as Target, West Elm, Dwell, and Japan's Uniqlo.

Arriving in the West in the 1990s, Uniqlo hit its stride with an affordable range of basic but colorful fashion, and in 2009 introduced its +J collection (designed by Jil Sander) in a very utilitarian color range of black, navy, and khaki plus a few seasonal colors. The down-to-earth look resonated with recession-weary consumers, and by early Spring 2010 the utilitarian trend, inspired by a retail concept, was showing up both on the runways and in the mall. Functional jackets, shirtdresses, and slouchy pants in a minimalist color palette were found in designer lines from Céline to Ralph Lauren to Rag & Bone and Phillip Lim, as well as in H&M, Next, Banana Republic, and Zara.

The utilitarian trend is a good example of inspiration—in this case coming from retail—finding its place in the zeitgeist. With the effects of the recession lingering, glamorous and extravagant fashion had become virtually unsaleable. Functional design in staple colors at an affordable price—the everyday mantra of Muji, Ikea, Uniqlo, and others—became the fashion direction of the season because it suited the existing social, political, and economic mood.

THE MEDIA

Finally, an easy and immediate source of information for color forecasters is the media. The daily newspapers, style magazines, retail catalogs, television, and many retail and fashion websites cover the constantly changing directions of fashion and lifestyle products. Fashion websites in particular, some free and some by subscription, provide nearly instantaneous coverage of the seasonal collections and runways, and fashion blogs have sprung up by the dozen. During the Fall 2010 collections a number of designers streamed their shows live on the Internet.

Every day is an opportunity to look around and ask "What is new? Why is it new? How does it resonate with what I already know?" Something that resonates is something that evokes a feeling of shared emotion or belief; the inspiration at hand somehow connects with our knowledge base and emotional intelligence—with the right side of the brain. As we observe, record, and interpret, the many inspirations began to add up. In *The Tomorrow People* Martin Raymond calls this **consilience** or consilient thinking, which he defines as "a 'jumping together' of knowledge, links, facts, ideas, theories, and insights from a variety of disciplines to form a new theory."

Design and color consultant Sandy McLennan of East Central Studios in London likens the process of working with color to "a whole kind of adult playschool that avoids rules all the way through—sometimes ending up with a mass of similar ideations, and that is either a sure sign you are onto something—or confused about something." The wealth of color inspiration can be overwhelming as well as stimulating. Listening to an inner voice—intuition—can help to make sense of it all.

Lagerfeld's bucolic fantasy at Chanel for Spring/Summer 2010 inspired color palettes that were quickly interpreted by chains such as Zara, Topshop, and New Look.

Dries Van Noten's Asian-inspired collection for Spring/Summer 2010 inspired colors and textiles for the mass market in turn.

Retailer Uniqlo's utilitarian concept—good design made affordable to everyone—has found its place in the zeitgeist, inspiring fashion at all levels of the market.

Marc Jacobs' Fall/Winter 2010 classic collection and quiet palette resonated with consumers during an uncertain economy.

INTUITION: THE INNER VOICE

The most creative artists and designers—those whose color palettes inspire us beyond their designated time and place—are those who break the rules. Robin Lane Fox, writing for the *Financial Times* about the letters and painting of Van Gogh, remarks that "a genius of an eye will see possibilities which rule books do not." While the theories of Michel-Eugène Chevreul (see p.73) inspired the use of color by the Impressionist painters, the post-Impressionist Vincent van Gogh listened to his "inner voice" and threw colors together that broke every rule of Chevreul's color wheel. Although van Gogh was not a commercial success in his lifetime, his intuitive use of color is now viewed as genius.

Intuition is that feeling in the gut that tells us something is so; it is insight that is quite independent of any reasoning process. Many designers and artists claim to rely on flashes of intuition or insight during the creative process. Marc Jacobs insists, "Over the years, I've learned to trust my instincts. Sometimes they're right; sometimes they're wrong. But I can sleep at night and always do a better job in the morning if I just go with my gut, my heart."

Designer Miuccia Prada is well known for disregarding the dictates of fashion and relying on her intuition. Her first commercial hit was a line of chic bags and backpacks using a military-spec nylon lining fabric from her family's luggage business. She continues to break the rules each season, mixing colors, unusual fabrics, textures, and prints in groundbreaking combinations.

Intuition is also the internal force that drives some people to style themselves in a unique and creative way, layering this scarf over that sweater over the printed dress over the ripped jeans or textured leggings. Fashion stylists working for designers, photographers, or magazines have a strong sense of intuition which they combine with research, often creating new looks that "bubble up" into a trend. (Although of course not all intuitive ideas lead to commercial success—often a truly brilliant or radical concept is simply too new to be accepted by consumers.)

It is important to acknowledge the role of intuition in the creative process, because in today's business climate designers and color forecasters are pressured to "rationalize" design decisions. Business managers usually believe that if something can't be counted, analyzed, or measured, it isn't real or doesn't have relevance to the bottom line. Because intuitive decisions cannot be quantified, intuition is often viewed as unreliable. But the inability to rationalize intuition doesn't necessarily make it wrong.

In *Blink* Malcolm Gladwell refers to that part of the brain that leaps to conclusions as "the adaptive unconscious" or an "internal computer." In the blink of an eye we know the answer to the question or the solution to a problem. Gladwell goes on to explain that our intuition is able to function in this way based on

Listening to his intuition, the artist Vincent van Gogh used color in a way that broke the established rules of color theory.

Designer Miuccia Prada has said she bases most of her decisions on intuition, using unusual fabrics and materials in unexpected ways.

our accumulation of experience or knowledge about a particular subject or situation. In other words, intuition is a skill that takes years of experience and practice to develop.

This holds true for the process of color forecasting. Nathan Sinsabaugh of Kristian Andersen + Associates, a brand and design consultancy in Indianapolis, points out that there may be times when a designer or color forecaster is right, just because they are right, even if their opinion flies in the face of cultural trends, color theory, and logical explanation. But keep in mind that this intuition or insight is based on years of experience and observation that allow the color forecaster to judge the rightness of the design decision, seemingly in the blink of an eye.

As the color palettes for Spring 2010 were being developed in 2008, hints of the coming economic downturn led many designers and retailers to choose colors from the safe end of the spectrum (see timeline on p.136). For the most part, the Spring 2010 store shelves and Fall 2010 runways reflected this, with utilitarian navies, khakis, nudes, and grays, along with classic, saleable brights. But some designers, taking a more intuitive approach, offered something bright, bold, and completely different; the PANTONE® Fashion Color Report Spring 2010 featured designers using turquoise, lemon yellow, scarlet and vermilion, coral and violet, and a range of eye-popping prints.

The intuition of a trained designer or color forecaster is a powerful force, and intuitive skills are well worth developing. On the other hand, the forecaster cannot expect a client to buy into a palette just because it "feels right." There must be a balance between the forecaster's expertise or innate knowledge, and the "story" or presentation developed to rationalize a new palette.

Designers and color forecasters have always relied on intuition and personal style. "One of our greatest gifts is our intuition," says fashion designer Donna Karan. "It is a sixth sense we all have—we just need to learn to tap into it and to trust it." As chairperson of the prestigious Design Academy Eindhoven, color and trend forecaster Li Edelkoort also speaks of the importance of intuition. "Believing intuition is also giving power and confirmation to your self-confidence. Most of the time we lose the intuition because we don't listen to it and simply discard it. But if we listen to it and research the reason, we can arrive to a greater solution."

An irrational idea—knitted cashmere cupcakes—is not necessarily irrelevant.

Our intuition relies on our accumulation of experience and knowledge, leading to insight, creativity, and the ability to problem-solve.

The visual memories of a childhood
in Algeria and his later home in
Morocco enriched the intuition of
Yves Saint Laurent.

The intuition we use to grasp abstract
ideas and inspirations, such as those
shown in this Masters of Linen's
"Linstallation" during the Paris
couture shows, is developed over time
and can help indicate "what's next"
to the observant forecaster.

DEVELOPING INTUITION

Most of us use both sides of our brains in learning and problem-solving. **Left-brain thinking** focuses on logical thinking, analysis, and accuracy. In right-brain thinking, we rely more on our intuition than on the analysis of facts and figures. While intuitive or right-brain dominance is partially a personality trait, it can also be developed as a skill. This takes time and patience, and benefits from a curriculum rich in the arts, visualization, metaphor, role-playing, creativity, and exploration. Edelkoort believes, "It's amazing, you can train the intuition like an athlete. The more I listen to my intuition the better I can perform."

Many design talents had the good fortune of a childhood rich in creative stimulation, with exposure to the arts or to travel and foreign culture forming a wealth of visual memories for their intuition to tap into. For Stella McCartney, this came from her father's music and her mother's photography; in the case of Yves Saint Laurent it was the exotic colors of his childhood spent in Algeria; a childhood spent in London's multicultural East End was filled with colorful and memorable stimuli for Alexander McQueen.

Most important, however, is the development of expert knowledge in one's field in order to develop confidence in the intuitive process. Years of experience or practicing one's craft can provide the color forecaster with a visual memory of what works, or doesn't work.

Color palettes and trends begin with intuition and inspiration; they are then confirmed by objective research and reasoning. Edelkoort confirms that "behind the intuition, there's also analysis, good sense, movement, evolution, and other rational things. But intuition remains the most important."

Intuitive skills, developed over time, can indicate "what's next" to the observant forecaster with a fine-tuned radar; but color forecasting is much more than just intuition. It requires a comfort level with color theory, color cycles, brand identity, target markets, and the discipline of research. A forecaster's track record, authority, and intuition are established over time; and one must practice the craft in order to understand its nuances and rhythms.

A REWARDING CRAFT

Combining knowledge, inspiration, observation, and intuition— thinking like a designer—the color forecaster's methodologies can perhaps be likened to a designers' version of the scientific method. "It's sloppy and messy and not nearly as disciplined as the scientist, but we do trial and error and we hypothesize and test and we see what we learn and then we go back and try again," explains Greg Galle, co-founder and managing partner of design consulting firm C2Group in Half Moon Bay, California, in Janet Rae-Dupree's 2008 *New York Times* article about design thinking.

Color forecasting is a craft that takes time, patience, and practice. Its reward lies not only in the fulfillment of contributing to the aesthetics of a product and the success of its retail sales, but in knowing that the consumer is purchasing the product because it satisfies their wants and needs. In addition, the knowledge acquired in practicing the vocation of color forecasting will enrich your appreciation and application of color in your own world throughout your life.

In Donna Wilson's studio we see color used creatively across a line of knitwear. Color forecasting contributes to the aesthetics of a product while promoting retail success by satisfying the consumer.

achromatic
Without hue; white, black, and gray are achromatic.

additive color theory
The combination of the three primary colors of light (red, green, and blue) results in white light.

alphanumeric
A system for referencing multiple items using both letters and numbers. Albert Munsell devised an alphanumeric system to designate colors by hue, value, and chroma.

aspirational fashion
The idea that consumers adopt the mode of dress worn by the upper classes in order to imply status, while style changes are driven by the upper classes in order to differentiate themselves from the masses. First theorized by Georg Simmel in 1904. See also trickle-down theory

Ballet Russes
The Russian ballet company, directed by Sergei Diaghilev, which performed between 1909 and 1929. Their radically new approach to dance, music, theater, and costume had a profound influence on the art and fashion of the day, particularly that of French couturier Paul Poiret.

bell curve
The bell-shaped graph of a color or trend life cycle, first demonstrated by Paul Nystrom in 1928, with time plotted on the horizontal axis and consumer acceptance on the vertical axis.

Belle Epoque
The "Gilded Age" at the beginning of the twentieth century, when the upper classes lived lavishly and fashion and the arts flourished. It came to an end with World War I.

brailing
As used by trend experts, it means tactile interaction with the world around us in order to soak up new ideas. First coined by Faith Popcorn as "social brailing", the term has been adopted by Martin Raymond.

brand identity
The distinct attributes that set a brand apart from its competition; it may include a signature use of color.

branding
The practice of assigning a trade name along with a set of marketable characteristics to a product or concept. Textile and fashion companies often invest in the branding of a generic product, e.g. Lycra® spandex (or elastane) or Trevira® polyester.

bubble-up theory
The idea that individuals looking to differentiate themselves from the majority influence fashion trends, with trends emerging from the "streets" to move up the social hierarchy, as opposed to trickling down from the upper classes. See also trickle-down theory

Chevreul's Law
See simultaneous contrast

chroma
The measurement of the strength or purity of color (absence of gray).

chromaticity
The quality of a color as determined by its dominant wavelength and purity, or chroma, represented by X + Z on a chromaticity diagram, while the Y value represents the value, or luminance, of the color.

chromaticity diagram
A model for graphing colors according to their wavelengths, established by the International Commission on Illumination, or CIE.

classic colors
Colors that are considered "safe" or always in style: black, gray, navy, red, khaki tan, white, and cream.

collective selection
Sociologist Herbert Blumer's theory that consumers make individual choices from competing styles through which collective fashion trends emerge, which express the zeitgeist.

color management system
A standardized atlas or resource for the visual communication of textile color standards. The best known are the Munsell color system, with its alphanumeric identification system for hue, value, and chroma; and the SCOTDIC and Pantone® color systems, which have each integrated a vast physical swatch system with computer software for digital communication of color standards.

color scheme
A combination of colors to be used together for a particular design or artwork. Color schemes utilize the complementary, contrasting, or analogous properties of colors to create harmonious or discordant effects.

color standard
The exact color desired for a product that has been agreed upon by the decision makers, and referenced via some standardized color matching system.

color temperature
Defined as warm (red, orange, and yellow) or cool (green, blue, or violet). Yellow and violet can be considered either warm or cool, depending on the undertone, which is the primary hue that defines a color's temperature. For example, violet can be warm, with a red undertone; or cool, with a blue undertone.

colorimeter
An instrument used to mathematically measure the colors of light in terms of hue, luminance (value), and purity (chroma); used in color matching.

complementary colors
In subtractive color theory, the hues opposite one another on the color wheel: yellow + violet, orange + blue, red + green. Combining two complementary colors results in gray. In additive color theory, combining complementary colors—cyan + red, magenta + green, yellow + blue—yields white.

consilience
Per Martin Raymond, the coming together of random knowledge, links, facts, ideas, theories, and insights to form a new theory.

cycle
A color or fashion cycle is a broad, long-term trend implying repetition in consumer preferences. Cycles become defined over time, following evolutionary style movement and existing for five or ten years or even a century.

design thinking
Defined by author Tim Brown as a collaborative process employing the designer's sensibilities and methods to match the consumer's needs with what is technically feasible and a viable business strategy. Design thinking includes "divergence," where choices are created, followed by "convergence" where decisions are made.

discordant colors
A color scheme that has broken from the natural order of color and appears unbalanced. A discordant color scheme is not always undesirable, but may be used for particular effects.

distributive network
Martin Raymond's term for a connected social or professional group of peers that is flattened rather than centralized, encouraging the flow of ideas, innovation, change, and newness.

fad
An ephemeral fashion movement, often bubbling up from the street and adopted by a particular market segment. Fads tend to be extreme with a short life span. Sometimes a fad becomes a trend, gaining popularity and entering the fashion vocabulary with help from the media and influential trendsetters.

FOB
Stands for "free on board," a term used in costing which means the product has been manufactured, packaged, and delivered to the vessel. This cost does not include shipping, landing, customs duties, or further transportation from the port of arrival.

gamut
In subtractive color theory, the range of colors that can be created by mixes of the three visible primary colors of red, yellow, and blue.

harmonic colors
Sets of two or more colors in relationships that are pleasing to the eye, loosely based on Itten's seven schemes of contrasting colors. Itten taught that colors used in balance would produce gray when mixed together.

haute couture
The design and marketing system authorized by the French government to create exclusive designs and bespoke fashion for wealthy clients.

hue
Any of the pure spectral colors we know by their color names: red, orange, yellow, green, blue, indigo, violet. They are produced by visible light of a single wavelength.

inspiration
Random exterior stimulation that helps drive the creative process, resulting in new ideas.

intuition
An interior insight or perception that is independent of any rules or reasoning process, based on instinct or gut feeling. The "inner voice."

light source
The source of light affects the way we perceive color. Daylight is considered a pure source of light. Indoors, fluorescent lighting is cooler (an absence of red) and incandescent light is warmer (an absence of blue). See also metamerism

market segment
A group of similar customers, such as executive women or weekend sport enthusiasts, within the whole of the marketplace.

mauveine
The first synthetic or aniline dye, derived from coal tar, created by William Henry Perkin in 1856. Less expensive and more colorfast than natural dyes, synthetic dyes revolutionized the fashion industry with color.

metamerism
In color matching, two colors that match under one light source, but do not match under another.

muse
A person who regularly inspires an artist, designer, or creator. Muses are usually female, in the tradition of Classical mythology where nine sister goddesses presided over the arts.

neutral
Technically gray, achromatic, or without hue. However, most grays have a warm or cool undertone related to the component colors. In subtractive color theory, gray is created by mixing two complementary colors: yellow + violet, orange + blue, or red + green. The definition of neutral has come to mean a combination of all three subtractive primary colors, which moves toward black, but becomes a muddy or earthy shade because the component hues are not pure.

palette
A set or range of colors used by an artist. In color forecasting, a palette may be seasonal or thematic, representing a forecaster's or designer's point of view.

pendulum cycles
The concept that fashion and color cycles swing from extreme to opposite extreme over a long period of time, and are influenced very little by individuals.

prêt-à-porter
"Ready to wear" or off-the-rack clothing, as opposed to couture or bespoke fashion. While the couture continues at a rarified level, designers now focus on showing their more profitable prêt-à-porter lines, which have evolved into today's semiannual Fashion Week shows.

primary colors
In subtractive or artists' color theory, those hues that exist naturally and cannot be created by mixing other colors: red, yellow, and blue.

primary colors of light
Red, green, and blue; the electromagnetic waves of light as perceived by the cones in the retina of the human eye. The combination of these creates white light.

printing primaries
While printing is based on subtractive color theory, digital media utilizes the colors of light. As color photography evolved, color printing was adapted to the primary colors of cyan, magenta, and yellow, the same as the secondary colors of light. Each printing primary (CMY) absorbs only one of the retinal primary colors, its opposing or complementary primary of light: cyan absorbs red, magenta absorbs green, and yellow absorbs blue. As each printing primary (CMY) is layered by the printer, the primary colors of light are absorbed, and the result moves toward black.

private label
A retailer's own brand, which may or may not be identified by the actual name on the label. Compared with independent brands which must be purchased by the retailer, private label merchandise carries a much larger profit margin for the retailer, and often has a shorter development timeline.

pure spectral colors
The colors of light conveyed by electromagnetic waves. Red, orange-yellow, green-blue, indigo, and violet are visible to the human eye (the visible spectrum), while the longer infrared waves and shorter ultraviolet waves are not.

retail assortment
A retail buyer will assort or specify the number of colors and percentage of each color ordered within a style or range of apparel.

retail brand
A brand that is sold only within its own chain of stores, catalogs, and websites. Retail brands generally control the design, manufacturing, and logistics of their own product.

retail classification
The appropriate use of a particular color in a particular season will depend on the classification or category of apparel or department within a retailer, such as outerwear, tailored clothing, knitwear, intimate apparel, and sportswear. These vary from country to country and retailer to retailer.

right-brain and left-brain thinking
Right-brain thinking relies on intuition and inspiration, while left-brain thinking uses logic, analysis, and accuracy.

saturation
The perceived intensity of a hue, paler or stronger under different lighting.

secondary colors
In subtractive color theory, these are orange (red + yellow), green (yellow + blue), and violet (blue + red).

secondary colors of light
Two primary colors of light can be mixed to form a secondary color. Red + blue is magenta, green + blue is cyan, red + green is yellow. When one of these secondary colors is mixed with its opposing or complementary primary—magenta + green, cyan + red, yellow + blue—the result is white light.

shade
A hue with the addition of black.

simultaneous contrast (or Chevreul's Law)
The combination of a hue and the color immediately to the right or left of its complement. The colors that appear together will be altered as if mixed with the complement of the other color, creating a feeling of vibration or liveliness. For example, yellow seen against blue will appear tinted orange, because orange is the complement to blue.

spectrophotometer
An instrument for the measurement of color via spectral analysis of the wavelength transmitted by an object without human interpretation. Spectral data is the most complete and precise means of describing a color, but calibration and metamerism can affect the results.

spectrum
Isaac Newton's description of the rainbow of colored light created by refracting white light with a prism; the Latin word for "appearance" or "apparition."

sportswear
A US term for modern dressing in smart separates that can be worn singly or in various combinations for business or casual activities. American sportswear emerged in the 1930s and 1940s. In Europe, the term has traditionally been used to describe clothing used for sport or athletic activities; this is more recently referred to as "activewear."

substrate
The raw material that underlies a fabric or component before it is dyed, printed, or otherwise finished.

subtractive color theory
As paint, pigment, or ink is added to a white ground, light is subtracted or absorbed, and the results get darker, moving toward black.

supply chain
The entire process of developing, manufacturing, and transporting a product for sale including its components, manufacturing operations, logistics, and shipping.

tertiary colors
In subtractive color theory, these are created by the mixture of one primary color with one adjacent secondary color from the color wheel. This means that a tertiary color is 75 percent of one primary color, and 25 percent of a second primary color. These colors are red-violet, red-orange, yellow-orange, yellow-green, blue-green, and blue-violet.

tint
A hue with the addition of white.

tipping point
A phrase borrowed by Malcolm Gladwell from Everett Rogers, it is the moment when a trend reaches critical mass and boils over into the general population, reaching peak popularity.

tone
A hue with the addition of gray.

trend
More enduring than fads, fashion and color trends are the result of cultural, social, political, and economic influences, lasting over one or more seasons.

trend chasm
Geoffrey Moore's term for the break on the upward swing of a trend's bell curve, a "black hole" where many fads die because they cannot make the leap into the mainstream.

trickle-down theory
The theory of fashion cycles first suggested by sociologist Georg Simmel in 1904. Simmel held that fashion begins with the upper classes, who are then imitated by the lower classes or "masses," causing the upper classes to buy into new fashions in order to differentiate themselves from the underclass.

tristimulus theory
The understanding that light is made up of energy vibrations of differing wavelengths, each representing one of the pure spectral colors. Objects themselves do not have color, but we perceive the color of the light reflected from them. The human eye receives these lightwaves through rods and cones in the retina. The rods convey gray, while the three types of cones perceive red-orange, green, and blue-violet light.

tristimulus values
The hue, value, and chroma of color as perceived by the human eye, expressed as X, Y, and Z on a chromaticity diagram.

undertone
See color temperature

value
The relative lightness or darkness of a color, determined by the amount of white it contains. A color with a high amount of white has a high value, or luminance.

visual merchandising
The way in which a retailer displays new trend stories and the merchandise for sale, including store windows, mannequins, shelves, and racks. Visual merchandising also includes print and Internet marketing.

zeitgeist
The spirit of the times; the general thought or feeling characteristic of a particular time, reflecting cultural, social, political, and economic trends.

FURTHER READING

Albers, Josef. *Interaction of Color*, New Haven: Yale University Press, 1963.

Ball, Philip. *Bright Earth: Art and the Invention of Color,* Chicago: University of Chicago Press, 2003.

Batchelor, David, (ed). *Colour: Documents of Contemporary Art,* London: Whitechapel Art Gallery, Massachusetts: MIT Press, 2008.

Birren, Faber. *Color and Human Response*, New York: Van Nostrand Reinhold Co., 1978.

Blaszczyk, Regina Lee. "The Color of Fashion," *Humanities*, March/April 2008, Vol. 29, No. 2.

Blaszczyk, Regina Lee. *Producing Fashion: Commerce, Culture, and Consumers,* Philadelphia: University of Pennsylvania Press, 2008.

Blumer, Herbert. "Fashion: From Class Differentiation to Collective Selection," *The Sociological Quarterly,* Summer 1969, Vol. 10, No. 3.

Brannon, Evelyn L. *Fashion Forecasting: Research, Analysis and Presentation*, 2nd edition, New York: Fairchild Books, 2005.

Bredenfoerder, Jack. "Color Strategy," *What's Up Below Deck? Thoughts on Brands and Branding from the People at Landor,* June 30, 2009.

British Colour Council. *Dictionary of Colour Standards,* London, 1934.

Brown, Tim. "What Does Design Thinking Feel Like?" *Design Thinking: Thoughts by Tim Brown*, September 7, 2008.

Brown, Tim. *Change by Design: How Design Thinking Transforms Organizations and Inspires Innovations,* New York: HarperCollins, 2009.

Bruzzi, Stella and Chuch Gibson, Pamela (eds). *Fashion Cultures: Theories, Explanations and Analysis*, London and New York: Routledge, 2000.

Busuttil-Cesar, Stephanie. *Red*, New York: Assouline Publishing, 2000.

Busuttil-Cesar, Stephanie. *White*, New York: Assouline Publishing, 2001.

Cassidy, Tracy Diane. "Personal Color Analysis, Consumer Colour Preferences and Colour Forecasting for the Fashion and Textile Industries," *Colour: Design & Creativity*, Society of Dyers and Colourists, Issue 1, 2007.

Clarke, Sarah E. Braddock and Marie O'Mahony. *Techno Textiles 2: Revolutionary Fabrics for Fashion and Design*, New York: Thames & Hudson, 2005.

Cleland, T.M. *A Practical Description of the Munsell Color System and Suggestions for Its Use,* Baltimore: Munsell Color Company, 1921.

Craik, Jennifer. *Fashion: The Key Concepts,* Oxford and New York: Berg Publishers, 2009.

Culatti, Veronica. "Emotional Dress," *Chromophilia*, March 28, 2007.

Cumming, Robert and Tom Porter. *The Colour Eye*, London: BBC Books, 1991.

Dawson, John & Jung-Hee Lee (eds). *International Retailing Plans and Strategies in Asia,* Binghamton, NY: International Business Press, 2004.

Delamare, François and Bernard Guineau. *Colour: Making and Using Dyes and Pigments* (New Horizons series), London: Thames & Hudson, 2000.

Diane, Tracy and Cassidy, Tom. *Colour Forecasting,* Oxford: Blackwell Publishing, 2005.

Eiseman, Leatrice. *Color: Messages and Meanings,* Gloucester, MA: Hand Books Press, 2006.

Eiseman, Leatrice. *Pantone Guide to Communicating with Color*, Sarasota, Florida: Grafix Press, 2000.

Feisner, Edith Anderson. *Colour*, 2nd edition, London: Laurence King Publishing, 2006.

Fesci, Sevim. "Oral History Interview with Josef Albers," *Archives of American Art*, Smithsonian Institution, June 22–July 5, 1968.

Finlay, Victoria. *Colour: Travels Through the Paintbox*, London: Hodder & Stoughton, 2003.

Fogg, Marnie. *Couture Interiors: Living with Fashion*, London: Laurence King Publishing, 2007.

Fogg, Marnie. *Print in Fashion*, London: Batsford, 2006.

Fox, Robin Lane. "Love, Not Anger," *Financial Times,* February 6, 2010.

Francis, Pat. *Inspiring Writing in Art and Design: Taking a Line for a Write*, Chicago: University of Chicago Press, Intellect Books, 2009.

Fraser, Tom and Adam Banks. *The Complete Guide to Colour*, Lewes, East Sussex: The Ilex Press Ltd., 2004.

Fukai, Akiko for Cooper-Hewitt National Design Museum. *Fashion in Colors*, New York: Assouline Publishing, 2005.

Gage, John. *Colour and Culture: Practice and Meaning from Antiquity to Abstraction*, London: Thames & Hudson, 1995.

Gage, John. *Colour and Meaning: Art, Science and Symbolism*, London: Thames & Hudson, 2000.

Gale, Colin and Kaur, Jasbir. *Fashion and Textiles: An Overview*, Oxford: Berg Publishers, 2004.

Gladwell, Malcolm. *Blink: The Power of Thinking Without Thinking,* New York: Little, Brown, 2005.

Gladwell, Malcolm. *The Tipping Point,* London: Abacus, 2000.

Goworek, Helen. *Fashion Buying*, Oxford: Blackwell Publishing, 2001.

"Guest Room with Color Expert Margaret Walch," *Special Events,* February 1, 2004.

Gutierrez de la Roza, Olga. *An Eye for Color,* New York: Collins Design, 2007.

Hornung, David. *Colour: A Workshop for Artists and Designers*, London: Laurence King Publishing, 2004.

Itten, Johannes. *The Art of Color,* New York: John Wiley & Sons, 1974.

Jackson, Tim and Shaw, David. *The Fashion Handbook,* Oxford: Routledge, 2006.

Jaeger, Anne-Celine. *Fashion Makers Fashion Shapers,* London: Thames & Hudson, 2009.

Jones, Sue Jenkyn. *Fashion Design, 2nd Edition*, London: Laurence King Publishing, 2005.

Kaiser, Susan B. *The Social Psychology of Clothing: Symbolic Appearances in Context,* New York: Fairchild Books, 1996.

Kendall, Tracy. *The Fabric and Yarn Dyer's Handbook: Over 100 Inspirational Recipes for Dyeing and Decorating*, London: Collins & Brown, 2001.

Kilroy, Jake. "Jake Finally Learns What a Color Strategist Does," *Entrepreneur Daily Dose,* Part I (February 20, 2009) and Part II (February 23, 2009).

Laermer, Richard. *2011: Trendspotting For The Next Decade*, New York: McGraw-Hill, 2008.

LaFerla, Ruth. "Fashion's Military Invasion Rolls On," *New York Times*, February 19, 2010.

Laver, James. *Costume and Fashion: A Concise History*, 4th edition, London: Thames & Hudson, 2002. First published as *A Concise History of Costume* in 1968.

Laver, James. *Taste and Fashion from the French Revolution to the Present Day,* London: G.G. Harrap & Co., 1946.

Lee, Suzanne. *Fashioning the Future: Tomorrow's Wardrobe*, London: Thames & Hudson, 2005.

"Li Edelkoort: The Business World's Trend Prophet," *Symrise,* 2007.

"Lidewij Edelkoort Interview," *Design Academy Eindhoven Source Program,* June 10, 2008.

Little, Jason. "On Trends in Design," *Landor's 2010 Trends Forecast.*

Littlewood, Glenn. "Effective Colour Communication from Mind to Market," *Total Colour Management in Textiles,* John Xin (ed), Cambridge: Woodhead Publishing Ltd., 2006.

Lowe, E.D. and J.W.G. "Quantitative Analysis of Fashion Change: A Critical Review," *Family and Consumer Sciences Research Journal*, Vol. 21, No. 3, 1993.

Lowengard, Sarah. *The Creation of Color in 18th Century Europe*, New York: Columbia University Press, 2006.

Lynch, Annette and Mitchell Strauss. *Changing Fashion: A Critical Introduction to Trend Analysis and Meaning,* Oxford: Berg Publishers, 2007.

Majima, Shinobu. "Generating Fashion Cycles: The Role of International Trade Fairs Since the Creative Destruction of Parisian Monopoly," EBHA Geneva Conference, September, 2007.

Martin, Richard. "American Ingenuity: Sportswear 1930s–1970s," *Heilbrunn Timeline of Art History,* Metropolitan Museum of Art, 2000.

Nemitz, Barbara (ed). *Pink: The Exposed Color in Contemporary Art and Culture*, Berlin: Hatje Cantz, 2006.

Nworah, Uche. "Decoding a Brand's DNA," *Brandchannel,* June 16, 2006.

Nystrom, Paul. *Economics of Fashion,* New York: The Ronald Press Company, 1928.

Pastoureau, Michel. *Black: The History of a Color*, Princeton, New Jersey: Princeton University Press, 2008.

Pastoureau, Michel. *Blue: The History of a Color*, Princeton, New Jersey: Princeton University Press, 2001.

Penn, Mark with Zalesne, E. Kinney. *Microtrends: The Small Forces Behind Tomorrow's Big Changes:* Twelve, Hachette Book Group, 2007.

Pesendorfer, Wolfgang. "Design Innovation and Fashion Cycles*,"* Discussion Paper #1049, Evanston: Northwestern University, 1993.

Polhemus Ted: *Street Style from Sidewalk to Catwalk*, London: Thames & Hudson, 1994.

Rae-Dupree, Janet. "Design is More Than Packaging," *New York Times,* October 5, 2008.

Raymond, Martin. *The Tomorrow People: Future Consumers and How to Read Them Today,* London: Financial Times/ Prentice Hall, 2003.

Robinson, Dwight E. "The Economics of Fashion Demand," *The Quarterly Journal of Economics,* Vol. 75, No. 3, August 1961.

Rogers, Everett. *Diffusion of Innovations*, 4th edition, New York: The Free Press, 1995.

Seivewright, Simon. *Research and Design*, Lausanne: AVA Publishing SA, 2007.

Simmel, Georg. "Fashion," *International Quarterly 10*, 1904.

Sinsabaugh, Nathan. "The Role of Intuition in Design Thinking," *Kristian Anderson + Associates,* December 3, 2009.

Smith, Paul. *You Can Find Inspiration in Everything* (*and if you can't, look again),* London: Violette Editions, 2010.

"Trend Spotting with Author Robyn Waters," *Business Week,* November 27, 2006.

Udale, Jenny. *Textiles and Fashion*, Lausanne: AVA Publishing SA, 2008.

Van Arsdale, Sarah with the Sheffield School of Interior Design. "Johannes Itten—The Art of Color," *Dezignaré Interior Design Collective,* New York: 2002.

Varichon, Anne. *Colors: What They Mean and How to Make Them*, New York: Abrams, 2007.

Vejlgaard, Henrik. *Anatomy of a Trend*, New York: McGraw-Hill Professional 2007.

Vinken Barbara: *Fashion Zeitgeist: Trends and Cycles in the Fashion System*, Oxford: Berg Publishers, 2005.

Waters, Robyn. *The Trendmaster's Guide: Get a Jump on What Your Customer Wants Next,* New York: Portfolio, 2005.

WWD. "Marc Jacobs Talks Style at WWD CEO Summit," *Women's Wear Daily,* November 17, 2009.

Zelanski, Paul and Mary Pat Fisher. *Color,* 6th edition, Upper Saddle River, New Jersey: Prentice Hall, 2009.

WEBSITES & BLOGS

www.always-inspiring-more.com

blog.entrepreneur.com

www.brandchannel.com

www.colormatters.com

www.colour-connections.com

www.cyanatrendland.com

designthinking.ideo.com

www.drapersonline.com

www.fashionclick.com

www.fashiontrendsetter.com

www.hintmag.com

www.landor.com

www.mintel.com

www.npd.com

www.nytimes.com/pages/style

www.retailforward.com

thesartorialist.blogspot.com

www.sensationalcolor.com

www.showstudio.com

www.specialevents.com

www.style.com

www.stylebubble.co.uk

www.tobereport.com

www.weconnectfashion.com

www.worqx.com

www.wwd.com

INTERNATIONAL COLOR ORGANIZATIONS

British Textile Color Group (BTCG)
See Intercolor

Color Association of the United States
www.colorassociation.com

Color Marketing Group
www.colormarketing.org

The Colour Group (Great Britain)
www.colour.org.uk

Comité Français de la Couleur
www.comitefrancaisdelacouleur.com

Deutsches Mode Institut
www.deutschesmodeinstitut.de

Intercolor
www.intercolor.nu

COLOR FORECASTING & TREND SERVICES

Carlin International
www.carlin-groupe.com

Christine Boland
www.christineboland.nl

Concepts Paris
www.conceptsparis.com

d.cipher fm
www.dcipherfm.com

The Doneger Group
www.doneger.com

East Central Studios
www.eastcentralstudios.com

Fordecasting
RoseannForde@aol.com

Huepoint Color
www.huepoint.com

International Colour Authority
www.colourforecasting.com

LA Colors from Amsterdam
www.lacolors.nl

Mudpie
www.mudpie.co.uk

Natural Color System
www.ncscolour.com

Nelly Rodi
www.nellyrodi.com

Pantone
www.pantone.com

Peclers Paris
www.peclersparis.com

Promostyl
www.promostyl.com

Sacha Pacha
www.sachapacha.com

SCOTDIC
www.scotdic.com

Scout
www.scout.com.au

Stylesight
www.stylesight.com

Trend Union
www.trendunion.com

Trendstop
www.trendstop.com

View Publications
www.view-publications.com

Worth Global Styling Network
www.wgsn.com

MUSEUMS OF COSTUME & FASHION

BELGIUM

Modemuseum Provincie Antwerpen
www.momu.be

FRANCE

Musée de la Mode et du Textile
www.lesartsdecoratifs.fr

Musées des Tissus et Des Arts décoratifs (Lyon)
www.musee-des-tissus.com

ITALY

Centro Studi di Storia del Tessuto e del Costume/Fondazione Musei Civici Venezia
www.museicivicivenezioni.it

JAPAN

Kyoto Costume Institute
www.kci.or.jp

SPAIN

Costume Museum (Madrid)
www.museodeltraje.mcu.es

UNITED KINGDOM

Fashion Museum (Bath)
www.museumofcostume.co.uk

Victoria & Albert Museum (London)
www.vam.ac.uk/collections/fashion/index.html

USA

Cooper-Hewitt National Design Museum (New York)
www.cooperhewitt.org

The Costume Institute/Metropolitan Museum of Art (New York)
www.metmuseum.org/works_of_art/the_costume_institute

The Museum at Fashion Institute of Technology (New York)
www.fitnyc.edu/3662.asp

FIDM Museum & Galleries (Los Angeles)
www.fidmmuseum.org

INDEX

Page numbers in **bold** refer to the picture captions

A
Aesthetic movement 100, 103, 104
Albers, Josef **66**, 68, 75, 77
All Saints 24
Alt, Emmanuelle 50
American Apparel 12, 30, 142
American Fabrics 50
Anthropologie 24, 150
Arcadia 144
art as inspiration 100, 102, 103, 104, 111, 168, **169**
Art Deco 103, 104
Art Nouveau 62, 104
Arts and Crafts movement 100, 104
Atmosphere **27**

B
bags 105, 155
Ballet Russes 62, 100, 103, 104, 168, **169**, 180
Bancou-Segal, Marielle 50
Beauty Bar **157**
Bedwell, Bettina 44
Belle Epoque 42, 62, 104, 180
Berry, Jos 58
Blaszczyk, Regina Lee 44
Bloomingdale's 24, 142
Blumer, Herbert 92, 180
Boden 12, 69
Bon Marché 24, 25
Bottega Veneta 114
Bowring, Joanna 110, 165
brainstorm boards **111**
brands 180
    brand identity 24–5, 26, 60, 118, 142, 144, 150, 180, 182
    and color forecasting 7, 12, 13, 22, 32, 33, 60, 63
    color relationship 12, 24, 25, 36, 118, 148
    in the supply chain 28, **29**, 30, 32, 33
Brannon, Evelyn 86
Bredenfoerder, Jack 86
British Colour Council (BCC) 44, 58, 82
British Textile Colour Group (BTCG) 57, 58, 117, 137
Brown, Tim 81, 108, 118
bubble-up theory 93, 180
Burberry Prorsum 96, **97**

C
Carlin International 44, 58
Cassidy, Dr. Tracy Diane 158
Castiglioni, Consuelo 114
catalogs 150, **151**
CAUS (Color Association of the United States) 44, **45**, 58
Chanel 12, 156, 170, **171**
Chanel, Coco 98, 100, **101**, 104, 152, 156
Chevreul, Michel-Eugène 68, 73, 74, 172
    see also simultaneous contrast
Chico's 118, 142, 158
Chloé **139**
collective selection 92, 180
Colombiatex 61
color
    analogous **78**, 180
    and brand image 12, 24, 25, 36, 118, 148
    chroma 67, 72, 74, 76, 77, **78**, 180
    classic 12, 24, 98, **101**, 102, 180
    color cards 42, **43**, 44, **45**, 47, 62
    communication 28, 30, 66–7, 68, 69, 74, 77, 80–3, 134 *see also* color management systems
    complementary 70, 72, 74, 76, 77, **78**, **79**, 181
    in context 152–3
    cultural differences 18, **19**, 36, **38**, 62, 104, 105, 145, 152
    emotional appeal **6**, 10, 12, 14, 16, 22, 36, 104, 105
    in history of fashion 36–43, 62, 100, 102, 104–5, 168, 170
    hue 67, 71, 72, 74, 75, 76, 77, **78**, 181
    limitations 154
    in marketing **6**, 7, 10, **11**, 36, 44, 63, 142–9, 158
    meaning 18, **19**, 36, 62, 104, 105, 152
    military colors 98, **99**, 105, 136, **139**
    neutrals 68, 76, **77**, 98, 105, **127**, **130**, 152, 182
    perceptions 18, 66, 68–9, 72, 75, 152, **153**
    primary 70, 71, 76, 182
    and printing 30, 71, 81, 100, 134, 182
    psychological appeal **10**, 14, 16, 22, 66, 104, 105
    secondary 70, 76, 182
    signature 25, 96, **97**, 98, **99**, 100, **101**
    standards 44, 57, 58, 68, 80, 180
    temperature 67, 72, 75, 76, 88, 180
    tertiary 73, 74, 76, 183
    undertones 67, 76, 88, **127**, 180, 183
    value (luminance) 67, 72, 73, 74, 76, 77, **78**, 152, 183
    see also color cycles; color schemes; color theory; color wheels
Color Association of the United States *see* CAUS
color atlas systems 81–2
color cycles
    bell curves 96–7, **128**, 180
    and color palettes 16, 26, 96, 98, 103, 128, **130**, 136
    consumers' role in 86, 92–5
    and cyclical events 98, 137
    defined 26, 86, 181
    in history 100–5
    length of 88–91
    timelines 104–5
    and tradition **97**, 98–9, 105
color forecasters 13, 16, 22, 108
color forecasting
    defined 7, **12**
    effectiveness 10, 16, 108, 158
    in history 36, 42–4, 62–3
    purpose 10–12, 13, **15**, 30, 178
color management systems 66, 80, 81–2, 180 *see also* Pantone; SCOTDIC
Color Marketing Group 12, **14**, **20**, 32, 57, 58, 117
Color Me Beautiful 158
color palettes 182
    and color cycles 16, 26, 96, 98, 103, 128, **130**, 136
    development 16, 26, 48, 96, 108, **109**, 125–35, 174
color schemes 75, 77–9, 180, 181
color theory 66, 70–5, 131, 172, 174, 177, 182, 183
    additive 70, 71, 180, 181
    subtractive 70, 71, 76, 181, 182, 183
color wheels **70**, **71**, 72, 73, 74, 75, 76–9, 131
colorimeters 80, 181
Concepts Paris 58
consumers
    color cycles role 86, 92–5
    emotional appeal of color **6**, 10, 12, 14, 16, 22, 36
    fashion role 86, 92–3, 94, 95
    personal color analysis 158
    psychological appeal of color **10**, 14
    purchasing and color 7, 10, **11**, 13, 158
    target customers 60, 118, **142**, 145, 158
cosmetics 12, 155–6, 168

CREDITS AND ACKNOWLEDGMENTS

Picture Credits

The authors and publisher would like to thank the following for providing images for use in this book. In all cases, every effort has been made to credit the copyright holders, but should there be any omissions or errors the publisher would be pleased to insert the appropriate acknowledgment in any subsequent edition of this book. (t = top, b = bottom, c = centre, l = left, r = right):

4: catwalking.com; 6: Andrew Meredith; 10: Kate Scully; 11 tl, tr, cr: Kate Scully; 11 bl: © Maria Tototoudaki/I-Stock; 11 br: UNIQLO UK Ltd.; 12 tr: Color Marketing Group; 12 bl: © Maria Toutoudaki/I-Stock; 13: SPINEXPO NY knitwear trends Autumn/Winter 2011–12. Photo: Debra Johnston Cobb; 14: Color Marketing Group; 15 t: Interfilière. Photo: Emmanuel Nguyen NGOC; 15 b: Interfilière. Photo: Debra Johnston Cobb, Garments made with Carvico fabrics; 16: Première Vision SA/Laurent Julliand, Stephane Kossmann; 17 t: Kate Scully; 17 b: Interfilière. Photo: Emmanuel Nguyen NGOC; 18: Kate Scully; 19 t: Photo: Kate Scully. The Cloth Shop, 290 Portobelo Road, London W10 5TE. 020 8968 6001 www.theclothshop.net; 19 c: EyesWideOpen/Getty Images; 19 b: Kate Scully; 20: Color Marketing Group; 21 t: Kate Scully; 21 b: Emmelia Cousins, references from Textile View – Womenswear S/S 2010, Fabric and Colour Forecast, Tim Walker, David La Chapelle, Galliano; 22 t: Image from 'The Cult of Nothing/Family Ties' section of PANTONE® VIEW Colour Planner, Winter 2011/12, 'Wonder'. Photo: Robert Roland. www.view-publications.com; 22 b: Image from the 'Programmed' section of Pantone-View Colour Planner, Summer 2011, 'Symmetry'. Photo and concept: Studio Gloria Jover. www.view-publications.com; 23 tl: Kate Scully; 23 tr: Jo-An Jenkins; 23 b: Robert Le Héros, Paris. Photo: Kate Scully; 24 t: © Tyler Stalman/I-Stock; 24 b: © Andresr/I-Stock; 25: Andrew Meredith; 26: Kate Scully; 27 t: Toast; 27 b: Associated British Foods plc/PR Shots; 28 t: © Crisma/I-Stock; 28 b: Pitti Immagine (Pitti Filatti 65), photo: Francesco Guazzelli; 29 t: Première Vision SA/Laurent Julliand, Stephane Kossmann; 29 cl, cr: Penn Textile Solutions GmbH; 29 b: Interfilière. Photo: Emmanuel Nguyen NGOC; 30 t: Margo Selby; 30 b: John Harrison, Design Director, Samuel Tweed Fabrics. Photography Lucy Harrison; 31 t, b: Donna Wilson; 36: © Frank van den Bergh/I-Stock; 37 t: © CAMERAPHOTO Arte, Venice; 37 b: Image supplied by the Society of Dyers and Colourists - Colour Experience; 38: Jan van Eyck, Portrait of Giovanni (?) Arnolfini and his Wife, 1434. National Gallery, London. NG186 © 2011 The National Gallery, London/Scala, Florence; 39: Kate Scully; 40: Private Collection/The Bridgeman Art Library; 41 t: Science Museum/SSPL; 41 b: Image supplied by the Society of Dyers and Colourists - Colour Experience; 42: © V&A Images/Victoria and Albert Museum, London; 43 t: Hagley Museum and Library; 43 b: © V&A Images/Victoria and Albert Museum, London; 45 t: The Color Association of the United States; 45 b: National Media Museum/SSPL; 46 t: Hagley Museum and Library; 46 b: Photo: Trevira GmbH; 47 l, r: Publisher: Lenzing AG Spring/Summer 2011. Trends: © MMgroup.uk.com; 48: CELC Masters of Linen by Vincent Lappartient; 49 tl, br: © Cotton Incorporated. All Rights Reserved; 50: Cover of textile VIEW magazine, issue 88. Photo: Phosphoresce by David Burton. The image relates to nature's radiance, inspiring creativity and scientific innovation. www.view-publications.com; 51: John Pratt/Getty Images; 52: Photo by Nat Farbman/Time & Life Pictures/ Getty Images; 53 tl, tr: © V&A Images/Victoria and Albert Museum, London; 53 b: catwalking.com; 54: Première Vision SA/Laurent Julliand, Stephane Kossmann; 55 t: Interfilière. Photo: Emmanuel Nguyen NGOC; 55 b: Première Vision SA/ Laurent Julliand, Stephane Kossmann; 56 t, b: SPINEXPO NY Color Trends Autumn/Winter 2011–12; 57 l: Kate Scully; 57 tr: PANTONE Colors; 57 br: Kensaikan International Ltd. Osaka, Japan is the publisher of SCOTDIC®; 58: Cover from Pantone-View Colour Planner, Winter 2009/10, 'Imagine'. www. view-publications.com; 59 t: Image from 'Imagine... and Dream' section of Pantone-View Colour Planner, Winter 2009/10, 'Imagine'. Photo and concept: Studio Gloria Jover. www.view-publications.com; 59 b: Image from 'Imagine... the planet' section of Pantone-View Colour Planner, Winter 2009/10, 'Imagine'. Photo and concept: Alex Giomo. www.view-publications.com; 60 t: These images are protected by statutes on copyright - Peclers Paris is the unique rights holder of these materials. Peclers Paris copyright; 60 b: UNIQLO UK Ltd.; 66: R.A. Smart. Photo: Kate Scully; 67 t, bl, br: Kate Scully; 67 tc: SPINEXPO NY. H. Stoll GmbH & Co. KG, Reutlingen, Germany. Photo: Debra Johnston Cobb; 67 b: Steven Bevis; 68: Poemo Design SRL. Textile Home Collections. Via Vico Necchi 56 22060 Figino Serenza CO Italy. All the products are made in Italy. Photo: Kate Scully; 69 t, b: Kate Scully; 70 r, 71 l, r: Steven Bevis; 72 r: © 2011 Photo Scala, Florence/BPK, Berlin; 73 t: Private Collection/Archives Charmet/The Bridgeman Art Library; 73 b: Science Museum/SSPL; 74: Steven Bevis; 75: Steven Bevis; 76: © DACS 2011; 77 l: Steven Bevis; 77 r: Paz Pur Alpaga. Photo: Kate Scully; 78 tl, cl, bl: Steven Bevis; 78 tr: Descamps. Gaelle Branellec; 78 cr, br: Kate Scully; 79 t, c, bl, br: Steven Bevis; 81 l, r: Kensaikan International Ltd. Osaka, Japan is the publisher of SCOTDIC®; 82, 83 t, b: PANTONE Colors; 86: 'The Pompadour' by Piers Atkinson AW/10, photographed on Lucy Atkinson by Morgan White; 87 t: Premium Bodywear AG; 87 b: Kate Scully; 88: www. breadandbutter.com; 89 tl, tr, bl, br: PANTONE Colors; 91 t: Associated British Foods plc/PR Shots; 91 b: © ranplett/I-Stock; 92: Photograph © 2011 Museum of Fine Arts, Boston; 93: Fotos International/Getty Images; 94 b: Getty Images; 95 t: 'The Empress of Everything' by Piers Atkinson SS/09, photographed on Rebecca Grover by Leigh Keily; 95 b: © ivanchenko/I-Stock; 96: Steven Bevis; 97 l: catwalking.com; 97 tr: Kate Scully; 97 br: © Warwick Lister-Kaye/I-Stock; 98: © Gino Crescoli/I-Stock; 99 l: Photo by Archive Photos/Getty Images; 99 r: catwalking.com; 100: Calmann and King, London, UK/The Bridgeman Art Library; 101 l: © V&A Images/Victoria and Albert Museum, London; 101 tr: Photo by Lipnitzki/Roger Viollet/Getty Images; 102 t: Photo by Caroline Gillies/BIPs/Getty Images; 102 b: Branex Design. Photo: Kate Scully; 103 t: SPINEXPO NY Knitwear

Trends Autumn/Winter 2011–12. Photo: Debra Johnston Cobb; 103 b: SPINEXPO NY. Photo: Nadav Havakook: Soft UPW; 108: © Izabela Habur/I-stock; 109 tl, tr: Amelia Williams, BA work; 109 b: Andrew Meredith; 110: SPINEXPO NY Color Trends Autumn/Winter 2011–12; 111: University of the Creative Arts at Rochester, Second Year Group Brainstorm Board. Photo: Kate Scully; 111 br: Photo: Kate Scully. The Cloth Shop, 290 Portobelleo Road, London W10 5TE. 020 8968 6001 www.theclothshop.net; 112 bl: Amelia Williams, BA work; 113 t: Sketchbook by Amber Rowe. Photo: Kate Scully; 113 b: Sketchbook by Amber Rowe. Reading Festival logo – Festival Republic. Bestival logo – Bestival.net. Photo: Kate Scully; 114, 115 l, r: catwalking.com; 116, 117 t: Kate Scully; 117 b: Color Marketing Group; 119: University of the Creative Arts at Rochester, Fashion Promotion Year 1, Group Project, Trend Analysis Workshop. Photo: Kate Scully; 120 tr, bl, 121 t, b: Kate Scully; 122–3: University of the Creative Arts at Rochester, Fashion Promotion Year 1, Group Project, Trend Analysis Workshop. Photo: Kate Scully; 124, 125 t, b, 126 t, cl, b: Kate Scully; 126 c: Teixidors®. Photo: Kate Scully; 127: Kate Scully; 128: catwalking.com; 129 t: Publisher: Lenzing AG Spring/Summer 2011. Trends: © MMgroup.uk.com; 129 b: SPINEXPO NY Color Trends Autumn/Winter 2011–12; 130 t: Kate Scully; 130 cl: SPINEXPO NY Color Trends Autumn/Winter 2011–12; 130 br: SPINEXPO NY Knitwear Trends. Photo: Debra Johnston Cobb; 132: Kate Scully; 133 t: SPINEXPO NY SANTONI Seamless Knitwear designed by Giovanni Cavagna with the Fashion Technology Dept. of Santoni. Photo: Debra Johnston Cobb.; 133 b: Color Marketing Group; 134: Kate Scully; 135 tl, tr, cl: LA Colors from Amsterdam/Lousmijn van den Akker; 135 br: Publisher: Lenzing AG Spring/Summer 2011. Trends: © MMgroup. uk.com.; 136: © Bjorn Meyer/I-stock; 139 all: catwalking.com; 142: © Radu Razvan/I-stock; 143: Kensaikan International Ltd. Osaka, Japan is the publisher of SCOTDIC®; 144: © Tomaz Levstek/I-stock; 145: Camper Together store by Konstantin Grcic (Verona); 147 t: Publisher: Lenzing AG Spring/Summer 2011. Trends: © MMgroup.uk.com; 147 tl: Interfilière. After Eden. Photo: Debra Johnston Cobb; 147 br: Interfilière. Gerbe Tights and Footless Tights OPAQUE 70. Photo: Debra Johnston Cobb; 148 l: © Angel Herrero de Frutos/I-stock; 148 r, 149 t: Publisher: Lenzing AG Spring/Summer 2011. Trends: © MMgroup.uk.com; 149 b: Ted Baker, London/PR Shots; 150: Andrew Meredith; 151 t: © Tony Tremblay/I-stock; 151 b: Sarah Maingot/trunkarchive.com. Toast; 152: catwalking. com; 152-3: Photo: Kate Scully; 153: Steven Bevis; 154 l: Interfilière. Photo: Debra Johnston Cobb; 154 r: Interfilière. Photo: Debra Johnston Cobb. Garments made with Jersey Lomellina fabrics; 155 t: Descamps. Gaelle Branellec; 155 b: Margo Selby in collaboration with The Old Curiosity Shop; 156 l: Image courtesy of OPI Products Inc.; 156-7: Kate Scully; 157 tr: Debenhams/PR Shots; 158-9: © Zeynep Ogan/I-stock; 162: Interfilière. Photo: Emmanuel Nguyen NGOC; 163: These images are protected by statutes on copyright - Peclers Paris is the unique rights holder of these materials. Peclers Paris copyright; 164 tl, tr: The Gateway School of Fashion, Pietermaritzburg, KwaZulu-Natal, South Africa. Photo: Kate Scully; 164 b: Photo: Kate Scully. The Cloth Shop, 290 Portobello Road, London W10 5TE. 020 8968 6001 www.theclothshop.net; 165: Sketchbook by Amber Rowe. Photo: Kate Scully; 166 tr, bl, br, 167 t, c, r: Kate Scully; 168: www.modeinfo.com. Mode Information GMBH; 169 t: © Len Kaltman/I-stock; 169 bl: Kate Scully; 169 br: © Duncan Walker/I-stock; 171 tl, tr, bl: catwalking.com; 171 br: UNIQLO UK Ltd.; 172: Vincent van Gogh, Two Children Strolling in a Park (Memory of the Garden at Etten). St. Petersberg, Hermitage Museum. © 2011 Photo Scala, Florence; 173: catwalking.com; 174: SPINEXPO NY Carol Edwards, The Knit Resource Center. Photo: Debra Johnston Cobb; 175: © Olena Chernenko/I-stock; 176 t: Photo by Adam Lubroth/Liaison. Getty Images; 176 b: CELC Masters of Linen by Vincent Lappartient; 178–9: Donna Wilson.

For all Pantone images: PANTONE Colors displayed herein may not match PANTONE-identified standards. Consult current PANTONE Color Publications for accurate color. PANTONE® and other Pantone trademarks are the property of, and are used with the written permission of, Pantone LLC. Portions © Pantone LLC, 2011. All rights reserved.

Authors' Acknowledgments

The authors would like to thank their color forecasting colleagues whose input was invaluable: William Benjamin, Joanna Bowring, Gaelle Branellec, Carole D'Arconte, Sue Chorley Fish, Elaine M. Flowers, Roseann Forde, Beryl Gibson, Gill Gledhill, John Harrison, Janet Holbrook, Mark McGovern, Sandy McLennan, Phil Patterson, Ellen Pinto, Laurie Pressman, Lindsey Riley, David Shah, Anna Starmer, Pat Tunsky, Lousmijn van den Acker, Pascaline Wilhelm, Lia Williams, Fran Yoshioka.

We also must thank Lee Ripley for her introduction to Laurence King Publishing, and acknowledge the expertise and patient guidance of our editors, Zoe Antoniou, Helen Rochester and Anne Townley, and the picture research done by consultant Emma Brown.

Debra Cobb would like to extend special thanks to Pat Tunsky for her introduction to this project as well as for her friendship and support over the years; and to Mick Siddons for understanding what this project meant to me.

Kate Scully would like to thank Jo-an Jenkins for her introduction to the project.

In addition, I would like to thank my colleagues and the students at UCA Rochester for their inspiration in learning and teaching. Finally, special thanks to friends, family and in particular Andrew Detheridge for their continuous encouragement and support.